YOUR
MIND'S
EYE

Important Note

The exercises in this book are the result of many years of working with people and are offered here in good faith. They are particularly suitable for healthy individuals who wish to sort out personal problems and understand themselves better; such people are likely to experience only positive results. Some of the recommendations, however, may not be appropriate for those in a mentally or emotionally fragile state, and neither the publisher nor the author can be held responsible for any untoward effects in these cases. People suffering from serious personal difficulties should always seek the guidance of a fully qualified professional in the first instance.

YOUR
MIND'S
EYE

How to heal yourself and
release your potential through
creative visualisation

RACHEL CHARLES

PIATKUS

In fond memory of my father,

who taught me how to appreciate the light and

shade of the imagination

Published in the UK in 2000 by
Judy Piatkus (Publishers) Limited
5 Windmill Street
London
W1P 1HF
e-mail: info@piatkus.co.uk

For the latest news and information on all our titles,
visit our website at www.piatkus.co.uk

A catalogue record for this book is available from the British Library

ISBN 0 7499 2048 3

Page design by Zena Flax
Edited by Rachel Connolly

Set by Action Publishing Technology, Gloucester
Printed and bound in Great Britain by
www.biddles.co.uk

Contents

Acknowledgements

First and foremost, grateful thanks must go to the dedicated and patient people who were my teachers, initially at the Institute of Psychosynthesis and subsequently at the Psychosynthesis and Education Trust, both in London. It was here, at the Trust, that I learnt the art of guided imagery. In particular I would like to mention Diana Whitmore, Piero Ferrucci, Judith Firman, Marilyn Feldberg, Nan Beecher Moore and Marilyn Kernoff, all of whom were a real inspiration to me. Next, I would like to express warm thanks to my co-trainees, who gave consistent support and encouragement while I undertook the adventure of exploring my own unconscious through creative visualisation.

Since then I have been privileged to work with a great many people who have been brave enough to confront their difficulties and find a way forward, often with the help of active imagery. While details of the case histories included in the book have of necessity been changed to preserve confidentiality, the psychological dynamics nevertheless remain sound, and I must therefore express wholehearted gratitude to my clients for providing me with the opportunity to understand the nature of the psyche at its deepest level. Indeed, I have often been awe-struck by the revelations that I have witnessed.

The visualisations described here are mostly my own invention, except for a few which are based on exercises that I learnt during my training. The origins of some are unknown to me, but where they are available elsewhere in a printed form, the references are supplied.

Gratitude is also due to my dear colleagues for their ongoing interest in this project, and for reading chapters of the manuscript and providing invaluable feedback. They include Ann Baeppler, Chris Hart, Peter Gleeson, Angela Hall, Anne Pickering, Maureen Luden, Barbara Dale and Marcia M.R. Oo. I would also like to express sincere thanks to Professor Petruska Clarkson for providing a group environment in which my own creativity has flourished.

My husband, John, has, as always, been wonderfully tolerant of my long absences due to the many hours spent tapping away on my word-processor. Moreover, he generously made himself available to listen to my ideas and could be relied on for an honest response. Our friend, Desmond Morrell, was also most helpful in introducing me to Yoga Nidra and lending me a precious book.

Finally, I offer my appreciation to my agent, John Pawsey, who saw the potential in my earliest thoughts about this book and helped to steer them in the right direction. My subsequent meeting with Gill Bailey and Sandra Rigby at Piatkus consolidated those initial thoughts. Without their enthusiasm and input this book might never have been completed.

Foreword

One morning I woke up and knew with certainty that I had to write this book. Why? Quite simply, as a counsellor and psychosynthesis therapist, I wanted to have it by me to give to my friends and clients, who constantly ask how they might use their own inner resources to heal themselves and to find personal happiness and fulfilment.

Only yesterday a colleague rang me in desperation: a close friend had, over the course of a week, and apparently without cause, completely lost her sight. Neither her doctor nor the hospital consultant could offer a diagnosis. Having lost the power to see the external world, she now wanted to focus on her inner vision. Could I help? Telephone advice seemed such a poor way of assisting; I so wanted to be able to send my colleague a book of hope that she could perhaps read to her friend to encourage and inspire her.

Others brought me similar requests. Cancer patients have asked about visualisation techniques to help send powerful self-healing messages to their bodies; some people have come to me suffering from extreme fear, stress, panic attacks or agoraphobia; others have difficult decisions to make and find themselves unable to move forward; while many clients are seeking a means of contacting their creativity. I know that I have only a brief hour each week to offer guidance, and that clients need to build their own inner reserves, need to have tools at their disposal that will offer strength on a daily basis and especially at moments of crisis.

Imagination is a wonderful human gift, sadly too little valued in our modern technological world. Yet we all have it within us, frequently lying dormant and just waiting to be developed to help us in our personal lives. In my work with people I have often been amazed by the images that they evoke, and heartened to witness their magical effect. I, too, have experienced the power of healing imagery when recovering from cancer, and have often tapped into my own inner wisdom when faced with personal difficulties.

This book, therefore, is the response to many requests, and the culmination of a decade of showing others how to develop and trust that truly remarkable faculty: the imagination.

Cransford, November 1999

Introduction

The world of the imagination. The gift of fantasy.
Visualisation: what it is. A word of caution.
The unconscious explained. How to practise visualisation.
Deep physical relaxation.

At just six years old I was suffering from night terrors. In those days we lived in an old house that creaked and muttered to itself, especially when the wind was up. Down in the cellar there was a deep well with inky black water, inhabited, I was convinced, by evil sprites that materialised after dark and invaded the upper storeys. As soon as the light went out I felt their eerie presence in the bedroom and now and again saw their weird, ever-changing shapes emerging from the darkness. Particularly menacing was a large monstrous being, whose one eye gleamed at me with a penetrating stare. Even worse was an amorphous creature with long tentacles that slithered its way over pieces of furniture until it reached my bed. At that point I would hold my breath, desperately hoping that it would fail to notice me and go away. The fear that the tentacles would seek me out and strangle me was overwhelming and I cowered under the blankets, too petrified even to call out. Finally I begged my mother not to put the light out until I was sound asleep As a compromise she lit a night-light for me and I was much comforted by the warm glow of the flame.

THE WORLD OF THE IMAGINATION

To small children, there is little apparent difference between fantasy and reality, and products of the imagination can have a powerful effect. Moreover not all infants have a sympathetic parent who will be reassuring and consoling. They may be laughed at for their 'stupidity', shouted at for being a nuisance or simply ignored. Sadly, such experiences can have long-lasting consequences, leading to a deep suspicion of the imagination, or even, in really chronic cases, to fear of closing the eyes.

At the other extreme are children who delight in creative play, finding a safe retreat in their make-believe worlds, apparently with few qualms concerning the fantasy creatures that may appear. Sometimes this acts as compensation for loneliness, and imaginative companions are created with whom conversations are held and games invented. Some youngsters are fascinated by anything ghostly or bizarre, enjoying the thrill of the fright.

Your personal reaction to the world of the imagination will depend as much on your temperament as on the environment in which you were raised, together with the attitudes of the adults around you. My mother was forthright and sensible, and a scientist by training, so dealing with the real world was her top priority. My father, on the other hand, had artistic leanings, ultimately becoming a self-taught water-colourist of considerable talent. I can still visualise him screwing up his eyes and contemplating the distant Lakeland hills, describing the subtlest shades of colour where only green or brown were visible to us. I was lucky enough, therefore, to be influenced by complementary approaches, at least as far as my parents were concerned.

Schooling, however, was mainly concerned with the learning of facts and the development of logic and verbal reasoning. Even poetry lessons were spent reading other people's works rather than creating our own, and art was considered to be a soft option, not for the serious-minded. I have no recollection whatsoever of receiving any guidance as to how I might contact my creativity, still less any encouragement to close my eyes and give free reign to my imagination. Was there a collective fear of monsters lurking within, that might be unexpectedly unleashed only to disturb the orderliness of boarding-school life? Whatever the reason, I grew up with the uneasy feeling that I was losing part of myself without knowing what that might be. Perhaps I even contributed to this process of repression, remembering only too well the night-time horrors of early childhood, with no wish at all to risk re-evoking them.

The gift of fantasy

Considering that many of the world's greatest inventions and discoveries have been brought into being through the use of visual imagery or even dreams, such systematic repression of unconscious material is a terrible shame indeed. Albert Einstein (1879–1955), for example, proposed the theory of relativity in 1916 as a result of fantasising what it would be like to ride on a beam of light. When explaining his thought processes, he said that words were not important, but rather 'psychical entities, certain signs and more or less clear images'. He emphasised the value of 'combinatory play' and added: 'The gift of fantasy has meant more to me than my talent for absorbing information.' It was in a reverie that Friedrich von Stradonitz Kekulé (1829–96), professor of chemistry, saw atoms whirling in a 'giddy dance', giving him a clue to the formation of his molecular theory. In 1865 a dream predicted an important discovery: this time the atoms twisted themselves into snakes and, as he watched, one of them caught its own tail. On waking he realised that the molecules of particular compounds were in the form of closed rings.

Further investigation of such experiences shows a crucial common feature: in order to open up to the imagination creatively, it is helpful to be deeply relaxed, either actually sleeping, a condition in which unconscious contents cannot be censured because the rational ego is no longer in charge, or in a kind of dreamlike state, a 'hypnogogic reverie', or perhaps just simply going for a walk .

Brilliant mathematician Jules Henri Poincaré (1854–1912) described how his moments of illumination came to him not as he was working away at his calculations, but rather after he had stopped. One night, having drunk some coffee, he lay half awake while ideas 'rose in crowds'. He explained how he 'felt them collide until pairs interlocked, so to speak, making stable combinations'. This raises another important point. Images are not always seen in perfect detail; they may be sensed in some other way, felt, heard or even smelled. With practice you will become familiar with your own individual way of receiving images.

If that is how the mind of a genius works, then why is it that Western culture, particularly as regards its conventional educational system, gives so little attention to the imagination? If only children were encouraged to work with images as well as words, then no doubt they would have a far better chance of realising their full potential. How much of this must lie dormant!

WHAT PRECISELY IS VISUALISATION?

The literal meaning of the word 'visualisation' is the experiencing of visual imagery in your mind's eye. In other words, it is your ability to picture people or things which are not present, either with or without your eyes closed, an aptitude which we all have to a greater or lesser extent.

In recent decades, however, the term has developed a broader meaning, due to its connection with the human potential movement and its employment in psychotherapy. With the power of your imagination, you can change those negative, limiting beliefs you hold about yourself into positive, life-enhancing images. With practice, as your actions follow suit, your relationships will improve, you will be able to achieve your goals and you can send healing messages to your body. Equally, images received from the unconscious can give you important information about yourself and advise on the most suitable course of action. Since memories are frequently stored in the form of images rather than words, the best way to have access to all that accumulated wisdom is through metaphor and symbolism. As you work through this book, you will discover how to use this non-verbal, intuitive part of your mind as a self-help tool.

Fortunately, it is never too late to learn how to tap into these inner resources, which can be used not only for creative or spiritual purposes, but also to assist in dealing with everyday affairs. Indeed, only in my middle years have I begun to appreciate what wealth lies in the unconscious. In my case it was a major health crisis that finally led me to understand what it was that I had been missing. Faced with cancer, I was determined to use every means available to assist with my own healing process, and meditation combined with visualisation became most valuable tools.

When I finally recovered, I realised that here were techniques that could be applied to all sorts of situations and I employed them to help me to reduce my stress levels, sleep more soundly, overcome nervousness and anxiety, and also to raise my self-esteem, all to good effect. Having had such positive experiences of visualisation myself, and having witnessed its impact on many clients, I know that it can help you too.

A word of caution

You may feel a little apprehensive about delving into the contents of your unconscious. Perhaps you were told as a child not to daydream, and this message may still be influencing you. On the other hand, you may be worried about meeting some monstrous beings, or about discovering certain things about yourself that you would prefer not to know. During many years of working with a wide variety of clients, it has become clear to me that defence mechanisms are very effective at protecting the psyche, and it is unlikely that anything will present itself to conscious awareness that you cannot deal with. This is not to say that this process is totally risk-free, because you may occasionally find some imagery alarming. You can, of course, choose to open your eyes and remove yourself from the experience whenever you wish. Take some deep breaths and feel your feet firmly on the floor. Alternatively, do not close your eyes at all; simply look at some plain surface such as the carpet or the wall. Nevertheless, if you sense that some of this inner work may be distressing for you, then do seek the help of a person trained in the technique, such as a qualified psychosynthesis therapist (*see* Useful information and Glossary).

Sometimes, in order to move forwards, it is necessary to feel the pain of the past – but afterwards you can be free from it for ever. The most likely aftermath of exploring your own personal imagery is that you will feel energised and liberated as you tap into creative potential, much more in control of your own destiny, and excited by the new insights that you will have.

WHAT IS THE UNCONSCIOUS?

Many people are puzzled by this word because it gives the impression that it is a definite object. It is obvious that we are unconscious when we are asleep or when in a coma, but what state are we really in and what exactly does this 'object' contain? This is a question that has been debated for centuries and is still under discussion. It often refers to the structure underlying human personality which the individual is not aware of, but which influences behaviour in innumerable ways. Speaking generally, it is the sum of all your experiences, feelings, thoughts, ideas and sensations, which you are currently unaware of but which have been stored in your memory, either for possible later retrieval, or in a repressed state to protect the ego. This includes not only everything that you were at one time conscious of, but also much that you have perceived subliminally or below the threshold of consciousness.

In other words, you have a vast amount of information stored in your unconscious which you don't know you have! A lot of this will be in the form of images rather than words. Just consider how much you learnt about the world during your first months on the planet, before you knew a single word, and then how much more followed while you still had only a very limited vocabulary. Such experiences are pre-verbal and can only reach consciousness via imagery or fantasy. Automatic bodily functions, and primitive drives and instincts such as sex and aggression, are all unconscious processes, whose psychological manifestations may or may not emerge into awareness.

Some psychologists and psychoanalysts also refer to the 'preconscious' which comprises an intermediate area between the unconscious and conscious regions. In other words, it is material that is ready to become conscious and therefore easily contacted by the aware mind. As I write this book, for example, I am drawing very largely on preconscious material, knowledge that is very familiar to me, having studied and worked with it for many years, although too great a store to carry in consciousness at any one time.

The psychiatrist Carl Gustav Jung (1875–1961) also believed that we are connected to each other via the 'collective unconscious' in the form of inherited mythological images that are common throughout our particular culture. Such images are often described as 'archetypal', and are found in fairy stories and epic tales. Examples are the witch, the earth mother, the goddess, the saviour, the hero, the wise old man, and so on. You may find these kinds of symbols penetrating your own consciousness through fantasy, symbolic imagery, creative play or the recollection of dreams.

It is difficult for our conscious selves to comprehend the vastness of the unconscious because we are only capable of focusing on one tiny piece at a time. As long ago as the seventeenth century, the philosopher Gottfried Wilhelm von Leibnitz (1646–1716) compared clear concepts to little islands rising above the deep ocean of obscurity. The exciting part about learning the techniques of meditation and visualisation, along with symbolic play, is that we can choose to have access to these profound seas of knowledge and use them for self-understanding, healing and creativity.

The idea of a 'superconscious' is also incorporated into some psychological theories, and is an important component of psychosynthesis. This area is usually regarded as a higher plane in an evolutionary sense, the home of our greatest aspirations and intuitions, the source of artistic, philosophical and scientific revelations and the spur to humanitarian action.

Sigmund Freud (1856–1939) considered that dreams were the 'royal road to the unconscious', whereby information about the self appears symbolically, and this is certainly an important route. However, day-dreaming or 'hypnogogic reverie' (a light trance, a state between waking and sleeping) can produce similar results but with the added benefit of staying personally in control. Play, in the form of artistic expression of some kind, such as drawing, modelling with clay, sandplay (creating landscapes with sand and small figures), writing poetry or fiction, dancing, singing or playing a musical instrument, is yet another way to connect with unconscious elements. Jung referred to this process as the 'active imagination', seeing it as a natural phenomenon, used spontaneously by children to gain some control over upsetting events. For example, a stuffed toy or doll, an imaginary friend or a pet, may be imbued with magical powers that will provide resolution, through dramatic re-enactment, to the real-life situation.

WHAT IF I CAN'T VISUALISE?

Some people are worried that no images will appear when they attempt to visualise. Such a concern may be based on a misconception that you will see an object in minute detail, just as if it were actually present. Some individuals do have this facility, but others just sense something. It doesn't matter at all how clear or faint the images are; you will be able to work with them whatever form they take. You may be one of those people who is more attuned to sound than sight, and therefore inclined to receive auditory messages. Perhaps you have a keen sense of smell, taste or touch and are mostly in tune with olfactory or tactile cues. If you have a special fondness for movement or dancing, then kinaesthetic sensations are likely to be meaningful. Your experience of the imagery will be individual to yourself, and may contain several of these elements.

It is extremely unlikely that you will be unable to receive at least a vague colour or shape. If you really do experience a complete blank, then ask yourself what might be stopping you from visualising. This could be fear of spontaneously reconnecting with some past trauma. In this case, just thank your mind for protecting you with such a secure defence. Reassure yourself that you are very efficient at erecting defences and that, at the moment, this is what you need to do. The more you value your defence mechanisms, the more likely you will be to trust them and therefore take the risk of letting them down at will. Wait a while, then start with a very simple exercise, such as the one below.

The lemon
Find a quiet place where you can relax, either sitting on a chair or lying down. Close your eyes, if you wish, allow extraneous thoughts to drift away, then turn your attention inwards.

*Bring into your mind's eye the image of a lemon.
Examine it in detail. See how yellow it is. Feel the
roughness and coolness of its skin. What does it smell like?
Take time to evoke it. Now place it on a chopping board,
take hold of a sharp knife and cut the lemon into quarters.
Put the knife down and look at the texture of the segments,
the shapes formed by the white pith. Now place a quarter
between your lips. Imagine biting into the fruit and
experience the bitter taste. Ugh!*

*Now gradually become aware of any physiological
changes. What has happened inside your mouth? Open your
eyes and be fully aware of your body. Has the amount of
saliva increased? Most likely it has – yet no real lemon was
present. This is a simple demonstration of the power of the
imagination.*

Were you able to see the lemon, or at least have some sort
of impression of it?

How to Practise Visualisation

It is helpful to divide the practice of the active imagination into different stages, and to take yourself through
these systematically. This provides a useful structure
for the work and will ensure that you will not miss out
anything. There are two main parts to the process: first
you let the unconscious come up; then you come to
terms with the contents received and put them to good
use. In my practice, I break these two main parts down
into subdivisions, as follows.

STAGE 1: PREPARATION

It is essential that you are not interrupted during your visualisation practice. Take the phone off the hook or put on the answering machine, place a 'do not disturb' notice on your door, and find a quiet corner where you can feel completely relaxed. You may have taped some of the fantasies from this book, in which case have your recording machine by you. Alternatively, ask a trusted friend or relative to read out the visualisations. This needs to be done slowly with plenty of pauses to allow time for the imagery to unfold. It is also a good idea to keep a journal of your experiences and insights, so have this to hand.

Sit on a comfortable, upright chair, that allows you to keep your spine straight. Place your feet firmly on the floor and let your hands rest naturally in your lap with open palms. If you prefer to lie flat on the floor, then this is fine. The only problem is that you might fall asleep! Give your weight up fully to the chair (or floor), close your eyes and take several deep, slow breaths.

Deep physical relaxation
Enter a state of deep relaxation by consciously tensing each muscle group, holding it for a few seconds and then letting it go. Breathe in as you tense, and breathe out as you relax.

Start with your feet and tense them by drawing your toes up and back. Hold, then let the toes drop. Move your attention to your calf muscles, and tense these by flexing your feet up from your ankles. Hold and let go as before. Repeat with the thigh and buttock muscles.

Follow the same procedure with the stomach muscles and tighten as if resisting a blow. After relaxing here, move up to the chest. Experience the deep relaxation flooding through your legs and torso.

Now clench the fists, hold and relax, then do the same with the other arm muscles. Raise the shoulders, then let them drop. Always keep up the slow, rhythmic breathing. Don't forget to clench and relax the jaw, then the facial muscles.

By the time you reach the top of your head your whole system will have slowed down and you will experience a warm glow.

If you are short of time, then practise a quick form of the above, which consists of tensing the whole body all at once, holding the tension, then relaxing fully.

Now clear your mind by putting any intrusive thoughts into a 'bubble' and watch this float away. Spend a few moments focusing on nothing but your breathing.

STAGE 2: CONTACTING THE UNCONSCIOUS

Now that you are deeply relaxed you will find you are in a receptive state. If you are working with a fantasy from this book, this will naturally lead you to the image or images that you wish to be in touch with. Having read the visualisation, you may be able to remember it well enough to go through it yourself in your imagination. If you have chosen to tape it, press the play-back button, using the pause control as appropriate. Give yourself plenty of time to evoke the images, to carry out the dialogues and so on. Anything is possible in this imaginary world, so don't be surprised if you find yourself having conversations with animals, or even objects! Just let the images come without censoring. Trust that your unconscious will supply whatever you need to know.

When the visualisation is complete, allow yourself to come back into the real world gently. If you experience any reluctance, then reassure yourself that you can return to the symbolic place or meet with the same images whenever you wish.

STAGE 3: EXPRESSION

Choose some creative medium through which you can secure and develop your fantasy symbols. Perhaps write about the images you have contacted, or else make some drawings or model them in clay. It is not at all necessary to be an artist, because it is the process of doing this that counts. Allow yourself to experiment. Some people like to create a landscape out of sand poured into a tray, placing small figures and toys (to represent people or things) into the scene as appropriate.

If you like moving, then step into the shoes of the characters you have met and explore them from the inside. Deepen your experiences and record them in some way, perhaps through poetry. Musicians may like to conjure up themes and improvise.

STAGE 4: INTERPRETATION

Only you can correctly interpret the meaning of your fantasy symbols, because the associations you have with them are exclusive to you. This was brought home to me most forcefully when I once reported a dream to a group.

The central image was of an old-fashioned mangle, which to me represented the way in which I felt that much of my vitality had been systematically squeezed out of me. To another member of the group, however, it signified clean, white laundry, a symbol of freshness and optimism – quite an opposite interpretation!

Look carefully at your drawings or models, or consider the memory of your images, and mentally take a step back from them and disengage yourself. Ask yourself questions such as: 'What occurs to me in connection with that?' 'How do I feel towards it?' 'What are my thoughts about it?' 'Does that figure remind me of anyone from my past or present life?' 'What are the main qualities present here?' 'What is the prevailing mood of the setting or landscape?' 'Is there anything missing?' 'What do I learn from this?' 'What meaning does it hold for me?'

You may have a number of significant insights.

STAGE 5: ETHICAL CHECK

Messages from the unconscious can be used for either good or ill. Hitler, for example, earned the reputation of being highly intuitive after a nightmarish dream saved him from a direct hit in the trenches during World War I. Be clear about your own values, those that are most meaningful to you, and use your critical faculty to judge how any new insights can best be incorporated into your life. In what way can the messages help you? Consider how they can be employed in the service of others.

STAGE 6: LIVING AFRESH

You now have to decide how newly released information and insights from the unconscious can be brought into your everyday life. Be specific and practical. Make a plan and set easily achievable goals, always taking the smallest steps first. Small successes build confidence. As you see, this is the stage in which you need to engage your will (*see* Chapter 7).

For example, one client had worked with a long fantasy during which she visited New Zealand, where she had experienced the thrill of white-water rafting. In reality she was a very timid person, attempting to break away from a dominating mother. The imagery had put her in touch with her repressed longings for freedom and adventure. When we considered the practical moves to take towards independence, she realised that, at twenty-nine, it was time to consider leaving home, but the smallest first step was to learn how to cook. So she volunteered to prepare weekend meals. By gradually taking on other domestic duties, she was putting herself more in charge at home. Eventually she felt confident enough to look for her own flat.

Stages 4 to 6 may not occur immediately. The true meaning of your symbols could take time to emerge and you may need to consider, over a substantial period, how best you can fulfil your dreams. Have faith that your intuition will reveal to you all you need to know when you are ready to receive its messages.

Chapter 1
Getting to Know Yourself

Tuning into your body, feelings and mind.

Observing yourself. Keeping a journal.

Meeting your subpersonalities and making friends with them.

Towards personal transformation.

Some people seem to know exactly who they are and what they want to do with their lives from adolescence on, following their chosen path with absolute certainty. I was reading about one such person recently, an author who had wanted to write since the age of sixteen. Unfortunately, no one seemed to be interested in his stories, which were the product of his bizarre imagination. Undeterred, he took casual, part-time jobs to keep the wolf from the door, and continued to produce novels. Finally, at the age of twenty-nine he took his latest precious manuscript to a publisher and luckily it found its way to an editor who immediately recognised its worth, and the book became a prize-winning success. Such persistence is rare, but staying true to yourself despite adverse circumstances is the key to the realisation of your full potential.

Most people, however, lack this certainty about who they are and what they want to contribute to the world. They muddle along through life, continually at the mercy of conflicting thoughts and feelings. At best, jobs and personal relationships end up as compromises. Some men and women suffer from deep feelings of alienation, always on the edge, never really sure how to include themselves; others are so deficient in confidence that they are unwilling to attempt anything new for fear of failure.

This chapter offers useful techniques for discovering your true nature. Aspects of your personality may not yet be available to full awareness, but the visualisations will activate your intuition, producing images that reflect your innermost self. As you learn more about who you are and experience the very essence of your being, you will find that you have far greater choice about how you wish to express yourself in the world.

BODY, FEELINGS AND MIND

My client settles herself in the chair. We exchange greetings and a little small talk about the weather, and then she tells me about her journey to my consulting room. As she does so, I notice how tense her body is and that, rather than sitting right back in the chair, she perches most uncomfortably on the edge. She is smartly dressed and I know from past interviews that she is successful in her career, but that she is suffering from chronic stress and has had a number of panic attacks. It is clear to me from her body language that her anxiety levels are high.

'How are you feeling today?' I ask.

The expected answer might be 'worried', 'rather anxious' or something similar, but she says: 'I was thinking on the way here that I'd like to talk about one of my work colleagues.'

I notice that in response to my question about her feelings, she has answered with a thought. I persevere and ask, 'What are your feelings towards this colleague?'

'She has a habit of withholding important information.' Once again no emotions are touched on, just a comment on the behaviour of this colleague.

'And how does that leave you feeling?'

I might anticipate 'annoyed', 'frustrated' or something along those lines, but she replies: 'I've asked her a number of times to keep me in the picture, but she takes no notice' – another thought, including an observation concerning her own behaviour, but still no information about her feelings.

I now deduce that this client is most comfortable in the area of thinking, and that either she is not fully aware of the difference between thoughts and feelings, or she is simply not yet ready to reveal anything that affects her emotionally. On the basis of this understanding I can choose to engage her on an intellectual level until it becomes apparent that she is more confident about exploring feelings.

Some people have great difficulty in telling the difference between thoughts and feelings and also body sensations. Learning to tune in to these three areas independently is a most useful way of getting to know yourself better.

To follow is an exercise to help you. There are three separate parts; if you have time, complete them in one day, or else spread them out over a short period. Read through them, then decide on the order. Notice in which area you feel most at home and which causes any discomfort.

Your body

Choose some music, something you particularly like which has a good rhythm, and put it on. Clear some space in the room and stand in the middle. Take a few moments to turn your attention fully to the sound and become aware of its impact on your body. Let yourself begin to move in response to the music, perhaps just swaying gently at first, until gradually a dance emerges. Develop your dance for as long as you wish, then return to the centre of the room and close your eyes, allowing your breathing to settle.

Now become aware of the type of music you chose. Was it heavy rock, jazz, classical? What was its mood? How did your body respond and what sensations were involved? Did you give yourself up fully to the beat, or were you rather restrained? Was it fun to move to the music or did you feel a bit silly or inhibited?

Focus fully on your body and the movements you made, then allow an image to form that represents your physical self. This may be a person, an animal or even an object. When you can see the symbol, take time to fill in the details, then hold an imaginary conversation with it. Tell it what you like or don't like about it. Hear its reply. Ask it what it most needs from you.

Allow the dialogue to come to a conclusion, open your eyes and make a drawing of your image. As you do this, become fully aware of your body, how you relate to it and what it most needs from you.

You may have been surprised by the image that your

unconscious gave you. When I first performed this exercise, my choice was some rather sleazy jazz and the image
for my body a sensuous long-haired cat. She was very
cross with me for neglecting her so badly and said she
needed to be taken better care of. I felt duly reprimanded
and made the commitment to myself to give more attention to the sensuous part of my nature.

Some people experience their bodies as awkward
and feel ill at ease inside them. Others may even dislike
their bodies. If, during the exercise, you have had this
type of encounter, don't be discouraged, but use this as
important information. Pay particular attention to whatever it is that your body wants from you and consider
how you might fulfil this need, starting with the smallest
step. Make some notes in your workbook.

Your feelings

*Find a comfortable chair and settle yourself into it. Spend a
few moments relaxing, close your eyes and take a couple of
deep breaths, then turn your attention inwards.*

*In your imagination, see yourself sitting at the dinner
table. Notice who is with you, or whether you are alone.
What are you doing as you eat? Chatting, dreaming,
reading, watching TV? As you see yourself, check in with
your feelings. Are you relaxed and happy and enjoying
your food? Are you perhaps feeling resentful or tired,
because you have done all the cooking and nobody seems to
be appreciating it? Or maybe you are glad to see others
delight in the meal you have prepared. Do you express what
you feel, or do you keep it to yourself? Do you have any
difficulties with eating? Just notice what happens, without
judgement. If you are on your own, you may be feeling*

lonely. Become fully aware of your mood, whatever it is.
How often are you in this state? Just be aware, without any
criticism.

As you connect with your feelings, allow an image to
form. It may be something recognisable, or just a colour or
shape. What are your feelings towards this image? Is there
anything you would like to express to each other?

Open your eyes and make a drawing of your feeling-
image. As you do this, check in with yourself. Does your
mood change at all during this process? Also notice your
body posture as you create your picture. What does this tell
you? Does this differ from, complement or reflect the feel-
ings in any way?

It is particularly important to complete the drawing if
difficult feelings were evident during this exercise, as you
may find that the expression of them on paper will help
lift your mood. Indeed, angry, hurt or painful emotions
are frequently eased through artistic expression. If a
client comes to me in despair, I often suggest that an
image is evoked from the feelings and a drawing made.
The result may simply be a blackened sheet, but just the
very process of scribbling with the crayon can help the
person to feel a little better.

Your mind

Choose a chair to sit in and close your eyes. Focus on your
mind. Now perform the following brainteasers, being aware
of your mental functioning. It is the process that counts
rather than correct conclusions, but curious readers will find
answers after the References.

a)   Visualise a square and a circle. Place the circle in the square so that it fits exactly.

b)   Twelve people crowd into a lift on the ground floor. It descends to the basement, two get out and one steps in. It ascends to the first floor, where six get out and two step in. At the second floor four get in and at the third ten get out. How many are left?

c)   Imagine a triangle made up of ten coins. There are four on the bottom row, three on the next, two above that and one at the top. Move just three coins to invert the triangle so that it points downwards.

d)   A bird is sitting on a perch inside an aircraft. If it takes off at the same time as the aeroplane, will the plane be lighter?

Do you enjoy your mind and like the way it works? Do you have an easy relationship with it or do you lack confidence when using it? How often do you criticise it and wish it were more effective?

Evoke an image for your mind, and visualise it taking shape. Talk with the image. Tell it about your feelings towards it. Hear its reply. Is there anything you would like from it, or it from you?

When the conversation is finished, open your eyes and make a drawing of the image. Write some notes about your mind.

When you have completed all three parts of the exercise, lay your pictures out in front of you, or pin them on the wall, and have a good look at them. Ask yourself the following questions:

1. Are all three areas – body, feelings and mind – readily available to me?
2. Which is most developed?
3. Where do I need to give more energy or permission for expression?
4. Which do I identify with most easily?
5. What is the relationship between the three?

Write the answers in your workbook and consider what you have learnt about yourself so far.

Over the next couple of weeks be conscious of the difference between these three areas and your thoughts and feelings towards each. At first just watch and notice, without being critical in any way. If you find yourself consistently in thought mode, then you might decide to pay more attention to your feelings and generate opportunities to be self-expressive. Be willing to take some small risks by putting out your feelings to others. (You will learn more about how this can enhance relationships in Chapter 4.) Consider including a creative activity in your life, such as redecorating a room, planning the garden, taking up dancing or singing, or learning a musical instrument.

If, on the other hand, you lack confidence in the thinking area, then encourage yourself to exercise your mind, perhaps by joining in discussions, doing some easy crossword puzzles, signing on for a language class – anything that will stretch your intellect. Congratulate yourself with each new achievement.

Don't forget that you inhabit a body! Be mindful of its needs and cherish it. It will appreciate your consideration and serve you well. If you are one of those people who has an uneasy relationship with your physical self, then you will find some of the visualisations in Chapter 3 helpful. Consider the remarkable complexity of the human body, the extraordinary ease with which the many systems work in cooperation with each other to maintain a healthy balance. Try and find the positive things about your body, anything at all that you like about it, and make a list. Work with these affirmations as described in Chapter 2.

OBSERVING YOURSELF

Make sure that you have your workbook by you at night time, so that you can write down some notes at the end of each day and so that you can describe any dreams in the morning. Before going to sleep spend a few moments reviewing your day and recording what you noticed, with the emphasis not so much on external events, but rather on your inner state. At what point were you in touch with your feelings? What did you do with them – bottle them up or express them? What was your mind engaged with? How was this for you? What was your body like – relaxed and efficient, or tense and painful? What changes happened during the course of the day? Some people prefer to begin their review with the evening, describing what their bodies, feelings and minds are like at present, and then working backwards. Whichever direction you take, notice in particular any patterns that recur. Also ask yourself if you have learnt anything new.

Your attitude when doing this exercise is crucial. It is not a re-experiencing or reliving of the events, but rather a detached observation of what happened inside you. Before writing, therefore, close your eyes and consciously adopt this position of observer, with an attitude of alert awareness. Your observing self does not criticise or make any judgements, but simply notices things with clarity and calmness. It is your observer who makes the notes at the end of the day.

THE INNER MULTIPLICITY

During the planning period for this section of the book, I had a most revealing dream which I would like to share with you. Most striking was an image of thin pieces of wood, approximately one metre in length, some of which were round and turned at the end, while others were square. They lay together on top of each other in a complete jumble, yet I had the impression that they had a purpose. If they were assembled they would form a useful whole, but the final shape totally eluded me. I half awoke, mentally fitting one piece with another in an attempt to create a meaningful object, but drifted off to sleep again without solving the problem. It was only some hours later when dawn was breaking that the answer came to me in a vision: I saw a staircase leading upwards towards a brightly lit area, and along the nearside of the steps were my pieces of wood, fitted together as the banisters!

It immediately occurred to me that the dream and its conclusion formed a perfect metaphor for the subject of this section: subpersonalities. We all have different aspects of ourselves that come into operation at various times, according to the current situation and our prevailing mood. Clusters of thoughts and feelings seem to belong together, and we may switch from one set to another, taking on that particular group of characteristics. Do not be alarmed: this phenomenon has nothing to do with schizophrenia or multiple personality disorder; it is a completely normal occurrence that happens to everyone, albeit at a more or less unconscious level.

Psychiatrist Roberto Assagioli, founder of psychosynthesis, observed this process, referring to the different clusters as 'subpersonalities', and developed the theory into a tool for personal understanding. It became apparent that each subpersonality had a strong emotional charge and was driven by a deep underlying need. He recognised that there were often conflicts between them, and that the way forward lay in accepting and valuing all parts of oneself, integrating even the difficult bits, to form a cohesive whole.

We often experience ourselves in a muddle, just like the pieces of wood in my dream. One part may wish to take one course of action, but another part disagrees, so we end up confused or immobilised. Getting to know the different pieces, to understand how they might fit together constructively, is each person's psychological task. Then it is possible to realise one's full potential, to be wholly oneself in the world.

It was noticeable that my staircase led from darkness up to light, as if embracing all of my being. As I watched, a cheerful little girl appeared and slid down the banister rail. I recognised her instantly. She was one of my subpersonalities, whom I have named 'Ragamuffin', the mischievous aspect of my nature, full of fun and bubbling over with energy. Contacting her has been crucial to my own development and personal happiness. There was a period in my life when I became a total workaholic and the spontaneous, joyful part of me became crushed, with the result that my health suffered severely. By inviting Ragamuffin back into my life a better balance was created and my wellbeing restored.

Meeting your subpersonalities

Now it is your turn to encounter some of your subper- sonalities and begin to understand who they are, how they operate, and what it is that they most need for themselves. One way to contact them is to begin to listen to your self-talk. Over the next few days take note of what you say to yourself. For example, first thing in the morning when you are trying to decide what to wear, you might encourage yourself by saying something like, 'How about that jacket? You look really smart in that.' On the other hand, a critical voice might intrude: 'No, don't put that on, it makes you look too fat.' Or perhaps you find yourself in a rush, berate yourself for oversleep- ing and tell yourself, 'Hurry up, or you'll be late!'

The first example might be representative of an internal Nurturer who cares about you, the second some kind of Critic that disapproves of you, and the third an Authority Figure that gives you instructions concerning your behaviour. Almost certainly you will find a small Child in you that feels vulnerable or unsure. Other common subpersonality figures are the Rebel, the Cynic, the Controller, the Trickster, the Sneak, the Victim, the

Mystic, the Martyr, the Witch and the Do-Gooder. Your own subpersonalities, however, will be exclusive to you.

Make some notes about your internal chatter and see if any themes emerge. Also observe which roles you take on in different situations. For example, a professional person such as a solicitor may put on a dark suit for work, representative of an earnest, responsible subpersonality. The corresponding body posture might be upright and briskly efficient. After work, however, the suit might be swiftly exchanged for colourful jogging trousers and T-shirt and a fun-loving, relaxed subpersonality takes over. At the weekend this same person may make a visit to see his or her parents and the well-behaved, compliant child comes to the fore, or an angry rebel may appear. Simply be aware of how you adapt yourself to different people and circumstances, how you feel inside, the body posture you adopt, the facial expression and clothes. At this stage, just observe and make notes, without passing any judgement.

Other clues to subpersonality figures can be found in the films, videos or plays that you watch, the books that you read, the works of art that most attract you or the music that best appeals. Which characters or famous people do you find yourself identifying with? Devote some space in your workbook for these descriptions.

It is very helpful to build images of your subpersonalities and to give them names, so that you will quickly recognise them whenever they appear. These images may be like real people or cartoons, or they may present themselves as animals, for instance a sensitive rabbit, a hedgehog with protective bristles, a dog that gets you out of trouble. Sometimes they may even emerge as objects, perhaps an evil computer, a hard-working engine, and so on.

You are likely to discover three or four central subpersonalities and approximately the same number of peripheral ones. Some people worry that they might be overwhelmed by a huge number of internal characters, but it is very unusual to exceed ten. The average is about seven.

After observing yourself for a week or two and making notes, it is time to invite your unconscious to allow you to contact your subpersonalities and get to know them better. The following visualisation will help you. Find a quiet place where you can relax, either sitting or lying down, but keeping the spine straight. After settling yourself, close your eyes and let go of all stresses and strains as described in the Introduction. Turn your attention inwards towards your deepest self.

The house in the wood

Imagine that you are in a meadow early in the morning. This is a pretty place where you feel at peace with yourself. The sun has just risen, some small birds are singing in the hedgerows, and wild flowers are opening their petals among the grasses. You wander around the meadow noticing its details and savouring the colours and perfumes.

After a while you see a path leading towards a wood. You have a sense that this is a very ancient place and you are curious to explore. Soon you are among the trees, and although the shade is deep, shafts of sunlight illuminate the way. You are aware of the sounds here, your footsteps crunching fallen leaves, and a small stream flowing by. Breathe in the atmosphere as you follow the path through the trees.

Eventually you find yourself in a sunlit clearing. You realise that you are standing in a garden adjacent to a house. Take a good look at the house. What is it made of? How big is it? How many doors and windows are there? Now you notice a sign on the building which reads 'Subpersonalities'.

You would like to meet the inhabitants, and, as the front door is open, you call out. Two of them appear and you invite one of them to walk with you for a while in the garden. What does it look like? How does it move? Is it friendly? What are your feelings as you look at it? Tell it what you feel. How does it respond? Find out what its name is and what its life is like. Ask it what it most wants for itself. Is there anything you can offer it? Continue the dialogue until you feel you know it a little better. Thank the subpersonality for meeting you.

Now ask the second subpersonality to come closer. How does this one move and what does it look like? Do your feelings change as you converse with this one, compared to the first? What are its particular qualities? Is there anything you would like to express to it? Ask it about its experiences and find out what its name is. What are its deepest needs? Would it like anything from you? As before, continue the dialogue until you have the information you want and thank the subpersonality.

You decide to wait here a little longer to see what happens. You sit on a garden bench and watch the two figures interact with each other. Do they get on well together, or are they quite hostile towards each other? Listen to what they are saying. What are your own feelings now? Consider whether you could offer them any advice. What might that be? Is there anything else you would like

to ask them or tell them, or that they wish to express to you?
When the interaction is complete, watch the two
figures go back inside the house, then say goodbye to this
place, knowing that you can return and meet your subper-
sonalities whenever you wish. Leave the garden and
re-enter the wood, following the path back to the meadow.
Once again appreciate the beauty and peace, then, when
you feel ready, open your eyes and return to reality.[1]

After finishing the visualisation, allow time to write out
the descriptions and dialogues in your workbook. If you
feel inspired, do a drawing of these two subpersonalities,
or model them in plasticine or clay. You can repeat the
exercise whenever you want to meet more of your inner
characters, or continue the conversations.

TOWARDS ACCEPTANCE

After some weeks of observing yourself you will be able
to recognise when one or other of your subpersonalities is
in operation. Become fully aware of the constellation of
thoughts, feelings and body language that constitutes
each subidentity and write a full description in your
workbook, remembering to include a name.

The next step is to find a way of accepting the
figures inside you, even if you dislike some of them. This
may be quite difficult. For example, you may have met a
coward whom you despise, or a critical school mistress
who makes you feel very small or afraid. Your instinct is
to deny these characters or push them away, but the more
you do this the more they will control you unconsciously.

Nevertheless, these are all aspects of your own psyche and they have been constructed for a purpose. As you come to know them better, you will begin to appreciate that they have their strengths as well as their limitations. Through acceptance the conflict and tension inside you will gradually reduce. The next exercise will help to deepen this process. I hope you will also find it fun.

Behind the masks

You will need cardboard or stiff paper, crayons, paints or felt-tipped pens, string and scissors. Have these by you.

Select one of your subpersonalities, then sit quietly with your eyes closed until you can visualise this character fully. In particular, see the facial expression, the posture, the clothes.

When you have a clear impression of this part of yourself, open your eyes and make a mask that represents it. If you can find or make dressing-up clothes to match, then so much the better.

Now put the mask on and consciously identify with and become this subpersonality. Adopt its posture and move around in the way that it would. Make appropriate noises, say in its own voice whatever it wishes. What is it like to be fully this part of you? Is it a strain, depressing, or delight-ful? What sort of world do you inhabit? Which situations bring you out? What are your predominant feelings? Are you happy, angry or afraid? Are you often in conflict or do you cooperate with other subpersonalities? What has made you like this?

Consider your limitations. Now do the opposite and connect with the very highest and best in you. What is your potential? What are your deepest needs? What drives you on?

What would happen if you took over permanently? What is
your name? Answer these questions in your own handwriting.
When you have fully experienced being this aspect of ·
you, consciously dissociate from it by taking off the mask and
any clothes, laying them down and stepping well back. Be
aware that it is only a part of you, then see if you can connect
with the centred place, the position of detached observer,
which is not a subpersonality. Look again at the mask and
know that you can choose to put on or discard this aspect of
yourself at will. This does, however, take time and practice.[2]

Now write about your experience and then repeat the
exercise with another subpersonality.

Remember to use your workbook each evening to
note down when the different parts of yourself were in
operation. Who or what triggered them into action? By
now you will be clear about the difference between
thoughts, feelings and bodily sensations, and you can use
input from these three areas to give you clues as to which
subself is present. Has there been a battle going on inside
you? If so, what has it been about? Perhaps one part has
wanted one thing and another part something quite different. Remind yourself that you can stand apart from these
aspects of yourself and take up a neutral, centred position.
This is the best place from which to make choices and decisions. (This is discussed further in Chapter 2.)

Most particularly notice the deep need that drives
each subpersonality. How is that need met – in a healthy
or destructive way? If the answer is negative, then
discover how you can fulfil the need more constructively.
For example, I have had great difficulty with a subpersonality I call 'Miss Whip'. She is tall and angular, wears

leather thigh boots, has a tightly buttoned jacket and carries a horse whip. She has a tendency to beat poor little Ragamuffin into submission, to tell her what a nuisance she is and how she wastes time. Her overwhelming need is to be in control, but while she ensures that I finish everything that I begin and perform tasks to a high standard, this can be at great expense to my health and happiness. The internal stress that she can cause is enormous. Knowing that this part of my personality wishes to exert control, I have deliberately taught myself to be assertive in my external life, to ensure that I achieve my ends, but in a healthy and productive way. She now no longer needs to control in a distorted fashion, because she can ask directly for what she wants in a firm but kind way. Indeed her whip is now mostly redundant. Her best qualities in addition to self-assertion are a strong sense of justice and willingness to stand up for it, along with an ability to achieve. She is also able to allow Ragamuffin much more space to be her fun-loving self.

Subpersonalities often evolve in pairs, in conflict with each other. So if you have contacted one, ask what its opposite is and another may well present itself.

TOWARDS INTERNAL HARMONY

As you come to know and accept your subpersonalities, you will find that they become more tolerant of each other and you will begin to experience a feeling of integration. Ultimately, your true, deepest self, which is not a subpersonality, will be in charge of the crowd within you and decide who is most appropriate for each different situation.

You may also resolve to give more space to those joyful, helpful aspects of yourself to achieve a better balance. Often this process is likened to an orchestra, with your real self as the conductor. Use the following visualisation to assist with this stage. As always, settle yourself first, relax fully and close your eyes.

The band

You are standing on the podium in front of a small orchestra or band, with a conductor's baton in your hand. This is a rehearsal for a concert and the music you are about to perform is harmonious, but as you observe the players you realise that it may be difficult to persuade them to play together and make the right entries. You recognise each one as a subpersonality, with the instrument of its choice. Take time to evoke them, to see which instrument each one has – a high flute, a low bass drum perhaps, a trombone or a harp – then what the body postures, the clothes and expressions are.

You wave your baton for the opening phrase, but soon you rap the stand requesting silence because of the grating cacophony. Few members are watching you and some are arguing: one or two are playing too loud; another is reading from the wrong music; yet another has forgotten to come in; others are far too soft. Just observe what occurs. It is your job to decide how each should play and to tell it when to make its entry. Solos can be shared equally. Most importantly the players need to listen to each other.

Visualise yourself in charge, making up your mind what to do and how to elicit the most harmonious sound from your band. Is there anything your players need to enable them to perform at their best? Have a dialogue with each.

It may be necessary to practise the piece several times over and repeat certain sections until the balance is just right.

After a number of adjustments your players are at last performing harmoniously. Enjoy the pleasant sound that they make for as long as you wish, then thank them warmly for their efforts.

If you are not familiar with the instruments of an orchestra, adapt the above visualisation to a pop concert in which your subpersonalities are the performers and you are the stage manager. See what happens! Record the fantasy in your workbook along with any thoughts or feelings you have.

Some weeks later repeat the orchestra or pop concert visualisation and check out whether there are any changes and if the players like each other any better and are more cooperative. Make notes about your self-understanding. Appreciate the qualities that your subpersonalities offer you.

TRANSFORMATION

Some subpersonalities may need extra help with their growth, especially those that are 'stuck'. The old behaviour patterns are so familiar that it can seem impossible to change them. However, the way forward is to allow yourself to be more fully yourself, rather than becoming something different. You already have everything that you need to be a whole person; it is a question of achieving good internal balance and allowing your full potential to be expressed. It is important to remember to embrace and accept all of yourself. When I first met my Miss Whip, I was embarrassed to admit that a part of me could be so unpleasant! After getting to know her better, I was able to appreciate her strong qualities and use those for my benefit. She was gradually able to loosen her hold on her whip.

There was another aspect of myself, however, a very fearful, panic-stricken part that could easily have sabotaged everything. One day I found myself in a crowded underground train, trapped in a tunnel. There had been a power cut and all the lights had failed, including, apparently, the emergency supply. I was aware only of unfamiliar bodies pressed up against mine and was overwhelmed with feelings of claustrophobia, desperate to rush out into the light and air, but knowing that there was no escape. To calm myself I used meditation and allowed an image to form for my panic.

Surprisingly a stuffed teddy bear appeared. He was bursting at the seams and had his paws over his ears and his lips sewn up tightly. I immediately felt sorry for him. He was unable to express his terror, or indeed anything. His deepest needs were for love and understanding so that he would feel secure enough to speak with his own voice. I decided to take him for a walk, and we climbed a gentle hill together. At the top I cuddled him tenderly and allowed my warmest love to flow into him. As I watched he took his paws away from his ears, began to smile and the stitches closing his lips dissolved. He jumped out of my arms, somersaulted around the hilltop, and sang at the top of his voice. I promised to look after him, especially whenever he felt confined and frightened, and we returned together down the hillside.

This visualisation enabled me to feel sufficiently calm until, to my great relief, the lights in the train came back on. Moreover, I had fulfilled Ted's deepest need by consciously giving him the love that he craved.

By allowing your subpersonalities to experience beneficial qualities, you can actively help them in their growth. Make up your own fantasies, offering them whatever they most need, such as courage, compassion, joy, patience, generosity, trust, serenity, wisdom, love or beauty. The following meditation can assist with transformation.

The lily

You walk into a beautiful garden with a chosen subpersonality. Spend some time with it here. It is a sunny day, and the garden is peaceful. The grass has been freshly mown and feels soft and springy under your feet. Trees offer cool shade, while the flowerbeds are vibrant with colour. Fill in the details in your imagination and notice how your subpersonality responds.

You find yourself particularly drawn to a pure white lily, still in bud but just about to open. The warm sun shines on both of you as you observe the bud while it gently unfolds its petals. The flower reveals its full beauty to you, radiant with light and scent. You invite your subpersonality to be open to the loveliness of the lily. See if there is any change. Have a dialogue together. How might you both bring the qualities of this lily into your life?

When the conversation is complete, you wander back through the garden with your companion. Is there any difference in your relationship, any new understanding?

Chapter 2
Outer Confidence, Inner Calm

Building confidence and self-esteem. Affirmations.
Creating a new vision of yourself.
Freedom from fear. Overcoming phobias. Feeling safe.
Help with insomnia. Making the right decisions.

Sarah was a young woman in her late twenties, who had come to see me because she was suffering from a chronic lack of confidence. With two small children, she spent much of the day at home, and even putting on clothes in the morning was a major problem because she could never decide what to wear, believing that she looked awful in every outfit. Sometimes it took her an hour or more to prepare to leave the house, as she tried on first one thing and then another. Nothing looked right. She was close to tears as she described her life to me. Even going out with her husband was difficult because she always imagined that the people they met were superior to her in some way. Either they were better looking or more interesting, or perhaps more socially at ease than herself. Her husband continued to be reassuring, but she found herself unable to believe him because she thought of herself as boring and ugly. She constantly feared that he would leave her for someone more attractive and intelligent.

In fact, the person I saw in front of me was not at all like her own description of herself. She had a slim figure, large grey-blue eyes and a tousled mop of thick brown hair. Moreover, she spoke fluently and had a soft, expressive voice. When the subject switched to her children, her whole face lit up and it was quite obvious to me that she was a most caring mother. Yet it was far too soon to share these reflections with her, as anything complimentary would simply be heard as a lie.

By the third session I felt that her trust in me was growing and it was time to work with some visualisation. I asked her to describe a recent occasion when this feeling of lack of confidence had overwhelmed her. She said it had affected her earlier that day when her mother-in-law had dropped in to see her. Sarah had been immediately aware of the smallest defects in the house, the toys on the floor, some washing-up by the sink, dust on top of the television, and had been engulfed with feelings of hopelessness and incompetence. I asked her to relax, close her eyes and allow herself to re-experience these feelings and to tell me what was happening, starting with her body.

'I'm no good, just hopeless. I'm shaky and trembling and there's a sick feeling in my stomach. I'm shaky all over. It's all too much. I just want to give up.' She buries her head in her hands.

'This shaky, trembling feeling, can you describe it some more?'

'It's very fluttery and light, but persistent – impossible to stop it.'

'What's it like? Can you get an image for it?'

'All I can see is a field of grasses. And now there's

one particular grass with fragile flowers that are being blown to and fro by the wind. It can hardly stand up straight.'

'Imagine becoming this grass and describe yourself.'

'I'm just one grass in a huge field. Totally insignificant. None of the other grasses take any notice of me. I feel lost and small. It's hard work just staying straight, especially when the wind blows.'

'And is the wind blowing now?'

'Yes, it's very strong and I'm bent right over. My flowers are shaking frantically.'

'What do you most need for yourself to help you feel stronger?'

'Warmth and nourishment.'

'Then just imagine that the skies are clearing, the wind is dropping and a shaft of sunlight reaches you. You are aware of its warmth on your stalk and you begin to feel a little better. You stretch your roots out under the soil and suck in the goodness. Gradually you are able to unbend yourself until you feel strong enough to stand up straight.' At this point Sarah removes her hands from her head and sits up. 'You nod to the other grasses and they nod to you. You feel accepted by them. You experience a sense of warmth and tranquillity.'

I give Sarah time to absorb these positive feelings, then tell her she can visit her field and re-experience this warmth and nourishment whenever she wishes. After this she opens her eyes and gently returns to the room. 'How are you now?' I ask.

'Calm.' She smiles.

In the discussion that followed I discovered that she

had been brought up in a large family in which there was little time for individual attention. She was frequently bullied by two elder brothers and had a sister who always gained higher marks than herself at school. She had adopted the habit of comparing herself unfavourably with the people around her and had totally lost sight of all her best attributes. I encouraged her to draw a picture of the grass as a symbol of herself and we considered its qualities. She was able to agree that it had a fragile beauty and that one of its best features was its sensitivity. This meant that she could empathise deeply with other people. Although easily bent by the wind, the grass never actually broke, indicating that she had reserves of inner courage and endurance. This work began to give her a new perspective on herself.

We then looked at how she could give herself and also receive the warmth and nourishment that she so desperately needed. Her self-image continued to improve over the ensuing weeks and she learnt how to parent herself in the same loving way that she looked after her children. At last Sarah felt worthy enough to accept her husband's genuine affection.

BUILDING CONFIDENCE AND SELF-ESTEEM

Many people come to me suffering from lack of confidence and poor self-esteem. If you are experiencing these problems, then follow the same process as Sarah:

Allow an image to develop for these feelings. Step into the image to experience fully what it is like from the inside, and in particular discover what its deepest need is.

Make a drawing or model of the image and learn as much about it as possible. Ascertain its very best, most useful qualities and fully appreciate these. Yes, it will have some! Then find a way of meeting that deep need in a healthy and positive way.

The image is, of course, a symbol for a part of yourself.

It is also valuable to identify any psychological benefits for remaining in that mode. It was such a painful place for Sarah that she was surprised when I asked her about this, but further exploration revealed that although she felt like a non-entity as her blade of grass, it was nevertheless a safe position to be in and a way of avoiding responsibility.

After some time Sarah returned to this image and saw that seeds had formed which were ready to be dispersed. This was symbolic of the way in which she was connecting with her new-found creativity, and her wish, at last, to make some significant contribution to the world in addition to motherhood.

The Nurturer

It is very important to be able to contact the caring part of yourself and to allow the Nurturer within you to develop. This part can then be used to attend to yourself as well as the welfare of others. If you were not securely nurtured as a small child this may be very difficult for you, and you will need to find a role model other than a parent, someone you know or have seen on television or read about whom you consider to be especially loving.

Take a photograph of this individual, cut out a picture or draw one, and tune in to their special qualities. What would it be like to be looked after by this person? What would you receive? See if you can give this to yourself, even in small amounts. Make a point of being with caring people.

Now see if you can connect with your own inner Nurturer. When was the last time you experienced a loving feeling towards someone, a feeling of wanting to do something for that person, or give a gift? Close your eyes and reconnect with that feeling. Allow an image to emerge for the caring part of yourself. This may come to you in the form of a person or animal, or perhaps an object or even an abstract shape or colour. When the image is clear in your mind's eye become aware of its details and qualities and what your feelings are towards it. Tell it how you feel. What do you most need from it? Make any request that you wish. Does it want anything from you? Are you willing to receive what it has to offer you? Does anything get in the way of this? If so, what kind of help do you need? Do you wish to say anything else to each other?

When your dialogue is complete, thank the Nurturer, then open your eyes and jot down some notes in your workbook. Do a drawing or create a model of your image and place it where you can see it frequently. Make contact each day with your caring part and be willing to receive what it has to offer you. Remember that whenever you feel unhappy or troubled you can call on your inner Nurturer for comfort and sustenance.

Affirmations

A good way to build a better internal image of yourself is to work with affirmations. These are statements about yourself that affirm that you are a worthwhile human being. Unfortunately, most people are only too ready to criticise themselves; when it comes to self-praise they find this extraordinarily difficult. Perhaps they have been admonished for being too vain or too big for their boots. It is sad that in our culture we are not encouraged to think well of ourselves.

In your workbook write down any agreeable, positive things that people have said about you, either recently or in the past. Now think of some personal characteristics or features that you genuinely like about yourself, starting with something simple, and add these to your list. Leave plenty of space for further additions as they come to mind.

Now write several on a card, make an attractive border, and pin this next to your mirror where you can see it each day. Make up a poem or song based on these affirmations, and say or sing it often. Become used to the idea of thinking well of yourself!

Some of the words that Sarah came up with initially were: good mother, nice thick hair, sensitive towards others' feelings, enduring, imaginative, soft voice, sense of humour. With prompting from myself she was able to extend this list considerably.

The ideal model

If you feel that you lack worth and have a poor self-image, it can be very helpful to build a different vision of yourself. This 'new' you will not be achievable all at once, but by holding the image in your mind's eye, you can gradually bring about the desired changes. When I worked in London in a high-stress job, my 'ideal model' was an older woman whom I had visited some years previously. She was a writer, living in the depths of the country, who had an air of complete contentment about her. She also had a delightful sense of fun. Modelling myself on her, I gradually developed a picture of myself standing happily at a cottage door in Suffolk, the wind blowing in my hair, my face covered in freckles and my arms filled with freshly picked flowers. As a compulsive workaholic and pale, strained city-dweller, there were a great many adjustments to make, both inner and outer, before such a transformation could be achieved.

Firstly, I had to let go of the obsession with work and give myself permission to relax and have fun. This was very difficult because my self-esteem had been constructed around work achievements; doing well at school had been my foremost means of gaining approval. As an adult it also had the distinct advantage of earning me a living, and paying for the mortgage and all the other bills, so my sense of security lay here. To sell my London house and move to the country seemed like an enormous risk, especially as my income would then depend on the uncertainty of freelance work. My happy country image nevertheless remained with me, and when the time was right I finally realised it.

Before creating a new vision of yourself, however, it is necessary to be aware of some of the traps. The following images will not help you to find your true self: 1) one that over-evaluates or, more likely, under-evaluates yourself; 2) an unattainable model, such as a glamorous film star; 3) the way in which you would like to appear to other people in order to receive something from them such as love or approval; 4) fitting into the images that others project on to you, i.e. models of what other people believe you to be; 5) fitting into the image of what other people would like you to be, e.g. your parents' ambitions for you.

When you come up with a fresh image of yourself, make a check against the above to ensure that it is not a false one. The type of image that you do want to build, which is based on your truest self, is the one that you really can become. The following visualisation will help you to connect with this.

Cast around in your imagination and bring into view someone whom you admire. This can be anyone at all whom you have met or heard about, either living or dead. If you are unable to think of someone known to you, then recall a character from a book or film that portrays qualities for which you have a deep respect. Evoke this person in as much detail as possible. How does he or she move around, stand or sit? What is the facial expression, the body language? What clothes are worn? What is the person doing? What kind of environment surrounds him or her?

Imagine yourself in this person's presence. How do you feel? What do you most like or admire about this individual? What qualities most attract you? If you would like some of these for yourself, then enquire how they have been attained. Ask the person for advice.

Now visualise yourself becoming that individual. Take a while to adopt the features and characteristics for yourself. What is this experience like? What is most unfamiliar or difficult about it? Does your body posture or facial expression change? Connect with any qualities which you wish to own yourself, and experience, from the inside, what it is like to embody these. Find a symbol for each quality.

Before returning to reality, affirm that you will bring these qualities with you. Now disengage from the admired person and identify with yourself again, having by you the symbols of the desired qualities. Thank the person and acknowledge that you can meet again whenever you wish. Visualise yourself owning the qualities and begin to see how you might express them in the world. How do you now appear?

Write about this experience and make a collage of your ideal model, together with images of its qualities. If feasible, find objects to represent the symbols and keep them with you as a constant reminder of how you wish to be. Evoke this person often to tune in with the sought-after characteristics.

Now make a realistic plan about how you might bring about the necessary changes. Begin with the smallest and simplest steps.

The 'acting as if' technique

Having discovered some of the qualities you would like to own for yourself, you can now begin to 'try them on'. The principle is that by adopting the behaviour and actions of the type of person you aspire to be, and by depicting the qualities of that character, you will actually give energy to those same attributes in yourself which require development. The appropriate emotions will follow the actions. For example, if we feel unhappy, the action of singing or whistling soon changes our mood – we act as if we were really feeling happy. It is difficult to be depressed while whistling. Try it! As a cellist I am often aware of how playing my instrument can change my mood for the better, especially if I'm initially reluctant. This technique does, however, require an act of will, but it will become easier with practice, especially as you achieve small successes. It is also helpful to adopt a playful experimental attitude. Become involved in the process rather than the outcome.

Bring into your imagination one quality you wish to develop or take on. Have you been in touch with this characteristic at a previous time? What was that like? Now visualise yourself with this quality. How does it affect your behaviour and your outward appearance? How do you relate to the people around you? Fill in the details until the image becomes real.

Frequently remind yourself of the quality by writing the word on a card and displaying it in your home. Practise adopting it privately first of all. When you feel sufficiently confident, try it out in the world. Do not be dismayed if you do not succeed immediately. Remember, this takes practice.

A new self-image

Now that Sarah was feeling much better about herself on the inside, she wanted to construct an external image that matched. She also enjoyed sewing, so here was an opportunity for creativity. After a number of discussions about the styles that appealed to her, she said that she loved to watch old 1930s movies, finding the dresses of that period softly elegant. I agreed wholeheartedly, realising instantly that the flowing 1930s lines were just right for Sarah's sensitive and romantic nature. After visualising herself in a pretty floral outfit and describing to me how happy she felt in it, we discussed the next, simplest step to take towards creating this new image: to go into town, look through some pattern books and choose a design that had a similar feel to it.

When Sarah finally appeared in her 1930s two-piece, she looked radiant. At last she was valuing her true nature and finding a way of expressing it.

Modern fashion may not be right for you either. Take a look at your list of affirmations and consider how you can emphasise your best qualities through your external appearance.

Use the 'ideal model' technique to conjure up a hero or heroine. What does this person wear? Imagine yourself stepping into those shoes. How do you feel? Make sure that the fit is comfortable in every respect. Consider the practical steps you need to take in order to realise your new image.

FREEING YOURSELF FROM ANXIETY AND FEAR

A famous violinist was performing a popular concerto. The hall was packed and the attention of the audience rapt as he plunged into the final movement at a spectacular pace. The passages became more and more complex, perspiration flew off his brow, and the orchestra was following helter-skelter. Just as he was approaching the climax of the work, a string snapped. The audience gasped, but the conductor kept the orchestra going. The soloist dropped his priceless Strad on to the stage, whipped away the leader's violin from under his chin and completed the piece in bravura style. At the end, the standing ovation was deafening.

When asked how he dealt with performance nerves, the violinist responded that he had thought deeply about all the most appalling things that could possibly happen to him, then, in his imagination, had devised strategies for coping with them. Breaking a string during a concert is one of the worst nightmares of any musician, but, because he already knew what he would do in this event, he was no longer afraid of it. He even turned this would-be calamity to his advantage.

Performance nerves

A great many people are fearful of any kind of public performance, whether in the glare of the spotlights on stage, delivering an after-dinner speech, standing in front of a class giving a lesson, speaking up in a meeting, or taking a driving test. It is well worth asking yourself what it is that causes your heart to race, your knees to wobble and your stomach to turn over. Generally, it is something to do with making a fool of yourself through a stupid mistake or saying or doing the wrong thing. Added to this may be a fear of the symptoms of fear, such as losing your voice at the crucial moment, or being unable to turn a page because your hand is shaking so much.

Perhaps you have suffered embarrassing moments in the past – for example, when a teacher shamed you in front of the class. In this case you may well be carrying an internal image of yourself as the object of derision, and you perhaps made some kind of resolution at that time never again to be visible in public. Such decisions are understandable, but they are also very limiting. As an adult you have far more resources for coping with an embarrassing plight than you had as a child, but because the painful situation affected you so deeply, you may not be aware of this. The following exercise will help you to change that limiting self-image.

I'm the one in charge

Take a few moments to recall a time when you felt deeply embarrassed or shamed in front of others. Bring the event into your mind's eye and see once again the situation, the people present and in particular the person who caused you to suffer. How old were you then? What had you done (or not done) and what was said as a result? How did the others react? How did you respond? What happened then? Did you make any decision that would enable you to avoid such pain in the future? How does this decision now limit you?

Affirm to yourself that you are no longer so young and inexperienced. You can now deal with such an occurrence differently. Evoke the situation once again and see yourself as you were then, but this time also include in the picture yourself as you are today. Tell your younger self that you are the one in charge. Thank him or her for reacting in the best way possible at that time and for looking after you, but that the responsibility is now yours.

Re-run the dialogue in your imagination, but this time from a position of feeling 100 per cent OK about yourself, rather than from the position of victim. Say now what you wish you could have said at the time, for example that it was an innocent mistake, that you have learned from it, that there was no need to make a public issue out of it, and request an apology. How does the person respond this time? What is the crowd's reaction? How do you now feel?

You may need to repeat this dialogue a number of times, seeing yourself confident and in charge and refusing to be put down or made an example of.

You will now be psychologically stronger and more able to cope with situations and events that might cause you apprehension.

I often wondered why I became so nervous before concerts, even as just one of several cellists in the orchestra. When I carried out the above exercise and took myself back in time I could see a pair of eyes staring at me which I immediately recognised as belonging to a particular teacher. As soon as these eyes appeared, I felt as if something withered inside me, as if all my confidence evaporated. As long as these eyes were gazing at me I was useless, no good. I therefore told the person concerned that I had had enough of being criticised and diminished by her, affirmed that I was a good cellist and always played to the best of my ability. No longer would I allow her to spoil my love of music. I then banned her from all future performances. Phew, what a relief!

The next time I was on stage I deliberately looked at the people in the audience, smiled at my husband sitting near the front, and affirmed to myself that no one was staring at me in a critical fashion. On the contrary, it was quite obvious that everyone was there to enjoy themselves. Now that I had banished my inner saboteur I could involve myself in music-making with a sense of wonder and excitement and without that terrible fear.

A small amount of nerves can be a positive experience before a performance as they will add extra sparkle. Too much tension, however, may well interfere. If you perceive a scenario as threatening, you may spark off the sympathetic branch of your autonomic nervous system to an unwanted degree. This 'flight or fight response' is vital in a genuinely dangerous situation and is part of our instinctive survival mechanism. If a wild animal were charging at you out of the African bush, then you would need that spurt of adrenalin to help you to sprint out of reach or shin up a tree. (You can read more about this in the next chapter.) Unfortunately, it is all too easy to set off this reaction in an inappropriate situation.

One good way to prevent this from happening is to do some deep, slow breathing prior to the event. This will counteract the flight or fight response by slowing down your heart rate. Deep physical relaxation, as described in the Introduction, will have an even more profound effect. Become familiar with the pleasant bodily sensations associated with this state until you can induce them at will. You may also like to meditate on a calming word such as 'peace'; just repeat it silently to yourself, allowing any intrusive thoughts to float away. You can support these exercises by summoning up an image of yourself in a totally relaxed state. Remember that it is physiologically impossible to be relaxed and tense at the same time!

Before any performance or test, always picture yourself doing well. See the smiles of approval and hear the clapping! Repeat this visualisation many times over.

The suitcase

A useful way of dispensing with unwanted nerves is to imagine leaving them outside the place where your performance or test is to be. Find an image for your nerves, take it to the door, tell it that you don't need it for the next hour or so and that you are going to shut it firmly in a suitcase. Picture yourself putting your image in the case and closing it. After the event remember to retrieve it, because you may genuinely wish to have the stimulus of your nerves in the future.

If you need an even more powerful effect, then make a drawing or model of your image of the fear, take it to the door and find somewhere to conceal it.

If I am feeling unusually edgy before a concert, I draw butterflies to represent that unsettled sensation in my stomach, and put the picture in my cello case where it remains throughout the performance! Afterwards I imagine them fluttering away. This is such a helpful process. Indeed, many of my clients have expressed huge relief at putting their fear outside themselves through some form of artistic medium.

Reassuring the inner child

Very often it is not your adult self who is afraid of a particular situation, but the small child who still resides in you.

Evoke your inner Nurturer, as described earlier in this chapter, and ask her or him to look after that little person. Picture the caring part of yourself telling the child that nothing frightening will happen and that you will protect it and keep it from harm.

If I am aware that my inner child has joined me on the platform, I hold an imaginary conversation with her, tell her that there is no need to feel scared, and ask her to sit quietly on a cushion by my side until the concert is over. She usually obliges!

Phobias

If you are suffering from agoraphobia (fear of open spaces), claustrophobia (fear of enclosed spaces), or other phobias such as arachnophobia (terror of spiders), dread of travelling, or if you experience panic attacks, then do seek professional help. Additionally, you can support yourself with visualisation.

One of the techniques adopted by behavioural psychologists when dealing with phobias is known as 'flooding' and involves gradually exposing the sufferer to the dreaded object or situation in a safe way until it becomes so familiar that the fear eventually dissolves. You can help yourself similarly by using your imagination.

Making friends with an object of dread
This project concerns a spider, but you can substitute any other feared object and alter the story accordingly.

Make sure that you are in a familiar, comfortable place and that you feel safe. Reassure yourself that nothing can harm you. This is purely an imaginative exercise and you can stop whenever you wish. You may like to wrap yourself in a blanket or hug a cushion or teddy as a security symbol.

Close your eyes and see yourself in a pretty garden. You are on holiday and feel relaxed and happy. There has been a brief shower, but the sun is now shining and the air feels balmy. You wander round the garden smelling the perfumes of the flowers. As you bend your head down to look at a rose bush you notice that there is a fine web stretched from one stem to another. Be aware of your feelings. Rather than responding with fear or rage, look at the web with curiosity, appreciating the intricacy of the pattern it forms. Some drops of rain glisten like diamonds on the web. You wonder what kind of spider has created something so beautiful.

After a while the owner comes to inspect its web. It is a most delicate little creature. In this fantasy world anything is possible. You can even have a conversation with a spider! Tell it how you feel and listen for its response. Ask it about itself and the life it leads. Get to know it. Ask it to promise never to cause you any harm. Focus on its best qualities and make friends with it. When you have finished your dialogue, continue exploring the garden.

You may need to repeat this visualisation a number of times, perhaps just seeing the web at first and meeting the spider later. Invent your own fantasies which incorporate non-threatening spiders in a safe environment. It is important to adopt an attitude of curiosity throughout. Pretend to be a scientist studying them. Learn as much as you can about these creatures from books and magazines. Cut out pictures and make a spider collage.

Eventually, when you feel safe enough to try this, put a glass bowl over a real spider, starting with a small one, and examine it. Ask a friend to be with you and look at it in a detached way. How does it move and how many legs does it have? What are its eyes like? Gather as much information as you can. Always affirm that it will never harm you.

Safe journey

The visualisation described below will help you to over-come travel phobias. If flying is not your problem, then substitute the mode of transport that is. As with prepara-tion for the above fantasy, make sure that you are safe and comfortable and have a security object near you, such as a teddy, cushion or blanket. If you feel nervous at any time, open your eyes and immediately connect with the comforting object. If possible, ask a trusted friend to lead you through the visualisation.

You are in the cinema watching a film which you yourself are projecting on to the screen. Be aware that you are in charge and can stop the film whenever you wish. The film is of yourself as a younger person and has taken you back to the time when you first felt fearful of flying. You see the event unfold, the people around you, what you say to them and how they respond. If, as you project this film, you experience any of your usual symptoms of fear, such as racing heart, dizziness or sweatiness, then press the imaginary stop button. Take some deep breaths, pick up your comfort object and steady yourself.

When you feel ready, resume the fantasy and press the rewind button. You are going to show the same scene again, but this time you will adjust the image so that it is smaller. If you like you can project it darker or in black and white only. Press the start button and adjust focus, brightness, size, colour, and so on, until you can watch it in reasonable comfort. Take your time, stopping again and making more adjustments whenever necessary.

After you have observed the scene all the way through without feeling panicky, congratulate yourself heartily.

Now you are going to show another scene. This time see yourself as you are now, a strong, competent adult. You are speaking to your younger self who experienced so much terror. You reassure him or her that it will never be necessary to go through such fear again. That is all in the past and you have survived the ordeal. You, the older, wiser person, are now the one in charge. If the original incident involved real danger, then it is natural to feel a little anxious, but being totally limited by fear is useless. Affirm that such a thing will never happen again. Make sure that your younger self really does believe this. When the dialogue is complete, the film fades.

The third scene is at a future date, when you may be faced with a similar situation. You see yourself once more, this time confidently climbing the steps to the plane. Check with yourself as to whether any symptoms are recurring. If so, stop the film, breathe deeply and relax before resuming. Adjust the image if necessary. See yourself enjoying the flight and arriving safely at your destination. The more often you can rerun such positive images the better.[3]

Phobias are in fact protective mechanisms in an extreme form. They are very effective in preventing you from having to face the feared object or situation again. So, it is best not to fight the phobia because this will only increase the tension. Rather, thank it for looking after you but tell it firmly that you can now cope on your own.

Even the symptoms of phobias can sometimes be very frightening, especially during a panic or agoraphobic attack. Having suffered from these myself, I know how terrifying they can be. There is an overwhelming feeling of impending disaster, you are likely to feel faint, there may be chest pains, inability to breathe properly, and fear of a heart attack or some kind of collapse. It is important to understand, however, that these symptoms are not in fact life-threatening, but simply the result of an over-sensitised nervous system. If you try and relax and stay with the experience, the alarming sensations will soon pass. Knowing that nothing terrible will happen to you helps to diminish the fear of the fear.

Find somewhere to sit down, if you can, and mentally transport yourself to a safe and tranquil place. The following visualisation will be helpful not only to phobia sufferers, but also to those who experience mild forms of paranoia.

Creating a safe place

Clients who experience fear feel reassured if they know that there is a safe place to retreat to in their imagination. It is somewhere comfortable and entirely secure. One client envisaged a warm room inside an impregnable fortress, another a tree-house, and a third a cosy cottage by the sea. Your image will be exclusive to you.

Relax, close your eyes if you wish. You are about to call to mind the safest place you are able to imagine. This is a place where no one can reach you or harm you in any way. When you are here you experience pure peace. Get in touch with feelings of tranquillity and safety and allow an image to emerge of a location with these qualities. Fill in the details in your mind's eye until you can see the picture clearly.

Now visualise yourself there. Experience fully how safe it is. This is a retreat, a resting place. Breathe in the atmosphere until you feel calm. Know that you can visit your retreat whenever you wish. It is always there for you.

Now make a drawing of your retreat and hang it on a wall where you will see it often.

SLEEPLESSNESS

O sleep! O gentle sleep,
Nature's soft nurse, how have I frighted thee,
That thou no more wilt weigh my eyelids down,
And steep my senses in forgetfulness?
(William Shakespeare, *2 Henry IV*, iii.1)

King Henry's throne is threatened and erstwhile friends are plotting against him. Whom can he trust? Fear has overtaken him, not just for himself, but for his kingdom. He envies his ordinary subjects their tranquil repose and concludes his soliloquy: 'Then happy low, lie down! Uneasy lies the head that wears a crown.'

Unease, anxiety and worry are major causes of sleeplessness. We go to bed with racing minds, turning a problem over and over hoping to find some sort of solution, but it remains evasive. Whatever it might be, it's best to write it down in a notebook before attempting to go to sleep. It is then 'off your mind' and on the page, so that even if no immediate solution is forthcoming, at least you can suspend it until the next day when you can plan some effective action.

The same applies to strong negative feelings. It is impossible to sleep if you feel very angry with someone. I clearly remember a time when I felt unfairly treated by a new boss. The job was just four months old and it had been a struggle for me to find my feet. The problem was a lack of a definitive job description, coupled with a resentful and uncooperative person in my team. My immediate superior should have made a written assessment of my work within three months, while I was officially on trial, but the appraisal had not been forthcoming. When it finally arrived, very late, it was devastatingly critical. I was shocked and extremely angry. Needless to say, sleep was impossible for nights on end, while I tossed and turned trying to decide what to do. Would I lose my job? Should I resign? Should I stay and fight my corner? What about the mortgage?

Finally it was Sunday night and a decision had to be made before work the next day. It was 2am and I dragged myself out of bed in a state of total exhaustion. Sitting down at the typewriter, I poured out my feelings in a tirade of indignation. As I wrote, it became clear to me that this man was in fact blaming me for his own shortcomings. I knew I had worked long and hard and that his criticisms were unjustified. Finally, I reworded my outpourings in a letter to him, with a copy to the director of the company. After that, sleep was forthcoming. Indeed, not only did I sleep well for the rest of the night, but my boss was reprimanded by the director and my job was safe. Moreover, I was treated with greater respect thereafter.

Once you have written down your worries, you need to suspend conscious, directed thinking to enter the world of dreams. You can use your imagination to help induce this state, by allowing your mind to wander freely, to drift into reverie. Being in a physically relaxed state assists with this process. Refer again to the Introduction for guidance.

A tranquil scene

Some people like to imagine looking out over a peaceful land-scape of rolling pastures, with grazing cows, the sound of a brook babbling by and softly rounded hills in the distance.

Take time to evoke such a scene. Picture the sun sliding down in the sky, the cows finding a warm place to sleep, settling their noses in the long grass, their eyes closing as they drift off to sleep.

While the counting of sheep is not to be recommended because this focuses the mind too much, imagining animals sleeping can help to put us into a similar state. As long as I have discharged worries or negative feelings into my bedside notebook, this always works for me. The animals I bring to mind are either our family dog or cat, whose ability to nod off at any time fills me with envy.

The sleeping animal

Think of an animal you know or remember, preferably one for whom you have feelings of affection. Call it to mind, imagining every detail, the colour and texture of its fur, its markings and its personality. See it moving around, playing, finally coming towards you and rolling over as you tickle and caress it.

The day is fine and balmy and you feel the warmth of the sun on the animal's fur. It stretches and yawns lazily. See yourself sitting by the animal and stroking it, being aware of how completely comfortable and relaxed its body is. Gently lift up a paw and feel how loose it is. You are aware that you yourself are beginning to unwind as you tune in to the animal's world.

You continue to stroke its fur with a gentle rhythm. Watch yourself doing this. Soon its breathing deepens and it falls asleep. You see how peaceful it is, with perhaps a slight twitch as it enters a dreaming state. Now your breathing also deepens and you know that you will soon fall asleep. Simply hear the regular breath of the sleeping animal until you do so.

Rock-a-bye-baby

Many of us were rocked to sleep as babies. Although we outgrew our cradles long ago, we can nevertheless recreate a similar sensation through fantasy.

Before sleeping, imagine yourself lying in a hammock attached to the branches of a tree that sways gently in a breeze. Alternatively, you may like to picture yourself in a boat that rocks soothingly on the waves. Allow yourself to experience the calming motion fully until sleep overtakes you.

HOW TO MAKE DECISIONS

The main difficulty that people face when trying to make decisions is that the various parts of themselves (or subpersonalities) have different points of view. One part will say one thing, another quite the opposite, while a third utters something else again, until the person concerned is totally immobilised. The best way to sort out this kind of inner conflict is to put each part on a chair in your imagination and let each have its say. You can then clearly see what is going on, take up the position of impartial observer, act as arbitrator, and make a truly informed decision from this disidentified place.

Hugh came to me asking for help with a major decision. Should he risk giving up his secure job as an art teacher to become a full-time graphic designer? I explained to him that it was not my job as a counsellor to advise him what to do, but that I could perhaps help him to reach his own conclusion. Firstly, I asked him to describe what he said to himself about this particular decision. He was able to distinguish a sensible voice that kept telling him to be cautious, a rebellious part that hated the school discipline, and the ambitious artist who wanted recognition for his talent. We set out four chairs. At that particular moment he was most in touch with the careful aspect, so he sat on one of the chairs and referred to himself as 'Sensible Simon'. He described himself as follows.

'I'm rather a worrier and tend to foresee all the things that might go wrong. If I give up my job teaching art then I may not find enough work as a designer to keep me going. I think it would be very rash to do that. It really is much more sensible to hold on to what I have. I may be bored by my work, but at least it's regular.'

I pointed out to him that he was sitting on the edge of the chair, his hands clasped in his lap. His lips were pursed and he frequently frowned. I asked him how he felt.

'I like to be in control and know where I stand ... but it's a strain. I'm not very happy.'

'What do you imagine yourself wearing?'

'Oh, a grey suit and starchy white shirt with a plain blue tie, and black lace-up shoes.'

'What is your deepest need?' I asked him.

'For security,' he instantly replied. 'That's very important.'

'What are your most useful qualities?'

'I'm very conscientious and hard-working and make sure that Hugh has a regular income.'

I then invited him to sit in a different place, and he chose to be the rebel. Instantly his body language changed. He lounged back, legs thrust out in front of him, hands in trouser pockets. He now described himself as a teenage boy called Robert Rogue and I noticed that his voice had much more energy. This boy wore casual jeans and a jaunty cap, and hated the school, especially having to discipline others.

'How do you feel towards Sensible Simon?' I asked.

'Huh, he's a pain in the bum. He's so po-faced. Never has any fun.'

When I asked Robert Rogue what he most wanted for himself, he jumped up, waved his arms in the air and shouted 'Freedom!'

The ambitious artist, called Kieron, was very different again, being highly imaginative. He wore a colourful patterned shirt, casual trousers and a gold stud in his left ear. He was fanatical about drawing and painting, excelled at typography and was good at coming up with original ideas. Given the chance, he felt confident that he could be a success. He got on well with Robert Rogue, but was in considerable conflict with Simon.

After an exchange of dialogue between the three, it was time to sit in the fourth chair and disidentify from these subpersonalities. Hugh realised that all of them were valuable to him in different ways. He wanted to accept the energy of Robert and the creativity of Kieron, while understanding that Simon helped him to keep his feet on the ground. If he gave up his full-time job, then Simon would suffer terrible pangs of insecurity. In the end Hugh decided to seek a part-time teaching job, meanwhile building up his freelance work until he felt confident enough to make graphic design his career. The rebellious energy could be absorbed creatively into his work by adopting a daring style. This way each part of himself could be satisfied.

Now it is your turn to put your subpersonalities on different chairs and let them have their say. (Before going ahead with this exercise, it is recommended that you meet some of them first by working through the appro-priate section in Chapter 1.) The stages of the process are as follows.

1) *Sort out the self-talk concerning the decision you wish to make. How many voices can you distinguish?*

2) *Set out the appropriate number of chairs, adding a spare one for the position of impartial observer.*

3) *Become identified with each subpersonality in turn. Speak as that person using 'I . . .' Describe yourself fully and be aware of your body posture. What are your feelings? What is your deepest need? What are*

your best qualities? Do you limit yourself in any way? How do you feel towards the other subpersonalities?

4) *Make clear what each subpersonality thinks and feels about the decision to be made. Become fully aware of the constituents of the conflict.*

5) *Sit in the place of impartial observer and arbitrate fairly between the subpersonalities. Can you make any recommendations from this position?*

The decision may not become clear immediately, in which case repeat the above process at a later date and note any changes. Eventually you will know what course of action to take.

Chapter 3
Glowing Good Health

Enhancing your immunity. Healing fantasies.
The power of love. Dealing with physical pain.
Soothing away stress. Sorting out internal conflict.
Understanding your body's messages.
Giving up smoking. The food that is right for you.
Making exercise easier. Celebrating your sexuality.

A sixty-one-year-old patient awaited a consultation with the radiation oncologist. The man had a serious form of throat cancer. His weight had dropped to 45 kg (7 stones), he could hardly swallow his own saliva and breathing was a struggle. His chance of survival was less than five per cent.

Fortunately for him the cancer specialist he was about to see, Carl Simonton, had been researching the influence that patients can exert over their own recovery, with encouraging results. With such a poor prognosis, the patient was only too eager to be a guinea pig in the study and agreed to follow the programme of deep relaxation and mental imagery that Carl recommended. He had to set aside up to fifteen minutes three times a day, and, after unwinding totally, imagine himself in a peaceful place, then evoke a symbol for his cancer. Next, he had to visualise his radiotherapy treatment in the form of millions of minute bullets of energy hitting the cells of his tumour. Because the cancer cells are weak and confused they will quickly die, while the healthy ones will survive. Then he had to imagine the white blood cells of his immune system swarming into the area, gobbling up the dead matter and disposing of it through his liver and kidneys. Finally he was told to picture his tumour much smaller until at last it disappeared altogether.

The efficacy of the radiotherapy far exceeded Carl's expectations, and the patient suffered few negative side-effects. The tumour receded, the man began to eat again and recover his normal weight and within two months he was in complete remission.

Medical colleagues were scathing about Carl's approach to cancer treatment, despite the fact that further research demonstrated that visualisation techniques could at least double a patient's prognosis, even in apparently incurable cases. At that time, in the 1970s, the scientific study of how the mind, nervous and immune systems are linked together, namely psychoneuroimmunology, had not yet been developed. Recently, however, it has been shown that the neurotransmitters, or chemical messengers in the brain, can communicate with the elements of the immune system. In other words, what you think and how you feel can directly influence the effectiveness of your immune defences. Of course it is common knowledge that if you are 'under the weather' you are more likely to suffer from infections, because your resistances are low. Conversely, we now know that immunity can be enhanced by sending it positive communications. Healing images can be a very powerful way of doing this and, whatever you may be suffering from, they can only be of assistance.

Enhancing your immunity

Like Carl's patient, you can help your immune defences to function more effectively. Whether you are suffering from a severe immune-deficiency disease such as cancer or AIDS, or whether you simply wish to avoid the onslaught of winter colds and 'flu, you can use your imagination to boost your immunity. In fact your immune system is amazingly clever. The white cells circulating in the blood and lymph are constantly on patrol, looking out for any foreign aggressors. Either they can produce a deadly chemical to destroy the invaders or else they can trap them and gobble them up. You can encourage them in their vital work.

After relaxing, evoke an image for any disease that you wish to fight. It's best to imagine the invaders as intrinsically weak. You know that your immune defences are stronger and have the power to overcome them. Allow a picture to form of your immune system, those clever white cells that can seek out any attackers and destroy them.

Picture your defences on patrol, alert to anything attempting to harm you. See them leaping into action and suppressing the invaders. You know how skilful and powerful your immune defences are. You watch as they overcome the enemy and are finally victorious.

Congratulate them and thank them for protecting you so efficiently. You can trust them to look after you.

My image when fighting cancer was of knights in gleaming silver armour charging about on white mares. They surveyed a hilltop (my breast) for any errant cells – these I pictured as wild mushrooms! Then I watched them spear the mushrooms and feed them to white goats who gobbled them up greedily.

To help protect my bones from secondary spread I visualised a strong tree, symbolic of my skeleton. My white cells were a flock of doves who investigated each branch for any black grubs (malignant cells). They pecked up those that they found and their droppings fell to the earth to fertilise the tree, which grew tall and healthy.

To reinforce the potency of my images, I made drawings of them. You may like to do the same.

Balanced immunity

Most people will wish to enhance their immunity. The exceptions, however, are those who are suffering from an auto-immune disease such as multiple sclerosis or rheumatoid arthritis. The reason for this is that the immune system has made a mistake and attacked tissue that belongs to the self, rather than to foreign organisms. If this has happened, you can help yourself by sending corrective messages to your white blood cells. For example, one MS patient fantasised that the elements of her immune system were students in a lecture theatre, and their teacher was explaining the difference between self and non-self. Another imagined that her damaged nerves were surrounded by protective blue light and could no longer be harmed. It is important that you create the visualisation that will assist with your particular disorder.

HEALING FANTASIES

Whatever you may be suffering from, general curative fantasies will be beneficial. One suggestion is that you create a place in your imagination which you can visit whenever you need healing.

The summerhouse

I often use this fantasy when under the weather. It provides me with a glorious feeling of renewal.

It is springtime, the bulbs have pushed up their shoots and are now in full bloom. You find yourself by a walled garden and you are very curious to have a peep inside it. You walk around until you find a small door in the wall. You press the latch and push it open. As you step inside, you have the impression that this is somewhere that is gently restorative. The scent of the flowers greets you, and as you wander across the lawn, you experience deep tranquillity.

In the far corner there is a summerhouse with a notice on the door saying 'Enter and be healed'. Full of anticipation you go inside and find a comfortable seat. You relax here for a while, watching the play of light creating beautiful patterns on the floor. You close your eyes and ask for healing. As you do so, a ray of sunlight breaks through the branches of the trees, filling the summerhouse with warmth and light. You experience yourself bathed in this golden healing light, allowing its gentle energy to permeate every aspect of your being. You imagine any hurt or diseased part of yourself being restored to health.

Feeling greatly renewed, you leave the summerhouse and the beautiful garden, bringing with you an object that

*will remind you of your healing experience. Take time to
find something of significance. You are aware that you can
return to this place in your imagination on any future
occasion.*

You may prefer to invent your own healing place. Take
yourself on the journey that is right for you and see yourself sitting under a restorative tree, perhaps, or in the
glade of a wood that has special powers.

Many people evoke water as a healing agent. One
popular fantasy involves following a river to its source
and finding there a curative spring or pool. The following visualisation also features water and can help to
relieve pain, wash away disease and provide a feeling of
wellbeing.

The shower

*When you feel fully relaxed, close your eyes and see
yourself in the most luxurious bathroom imaginable. There
is a deep-pile carpet on the floor, the softest of towels hang
from heated rails and gold taps gleam in the candlelight.
The walls are beautifully painted with fantasy murals, and
exotic plants grow in large terracotta pots. Steps, flanked
by ornamental pillars, lead upwards to the spacious bathing
and shower areas.*

*You have come here for rest, refreshment and healing.
Take a while to absorb the soothing atmosphere. You feel
warm and decide to have a shower, so you take off your
clothes, walk up the steps and draw back the curtains. As
you stand under it, the shower adjusts itself automatically
to exactly the right temperature and your skin tingles
pleasurably as the droplets of water run down your body.*

This is no ordinary shower: its special spa water has the power to relieve any aches and pains, to remedy any sickness, and to cleanse and refresh every cell in your body. Stay under this soothing, healing shower for as long as you need to and, as it washes over you, imagine it cleansing and revitalising every area of your being.

When you feel refreshed and renewed, step out of the shower, wrap yourself in a large, luxuriant towel and relax for a while. It will soon be time to return to the world, but before opening your eyes, remind yourself that you can come back here for healing whenever you wish.

THE HEALING POWER OF LOVE

Several men and women were watching romantic movies. They were subjects in a research project designed to test whether feelings of love could have any effect on their ability to resist infections. It is well known that people who are in love have fewer colds. Something seems to happen to our bodies when we experience those warm feelings. What is it? After the romantic movies had ended, saliva from each audience member was tested. Amazingly, levels of immunoglobulin-A had increased (this is the first line of defence against infections), and the effect lasted for up to an hour. Then the subjects were encouraged to recall times when they experienced receiving love. Here again, this gave a measurable boost to their bodies' defences.

This means that you, too, can stimulate your own healing energies, simply by reconnecting with loving feelings.

Love's healing energy

Evoke a healing sanctuary, a place where you feel totally at peace and in tune with restorative energies. Either create your own fantasy or use an idea from the book. See yourself comfortably at ease in this place.

Now recall a time when someone gave you tender loving care. (Alternatively remind yourself of your feelings when offering love to a person or animal.) What was the situation, the atmosphere? Who was there? Re-experience this as vividly as possible, focusing particularly on the quality of that loving energy. What is that like?

Allow an image to form of the loving energy, knowing that it has the power to heal. What colour is it? Does it have a particular shape, sound or perfume? Visualise any sore or hurt part of yourself tenderly caressed by love's healing energy. Now see this curative power spread throughout your entire body. Absorb this for as long as you wish.

Assure yourself that you can return to your sanctuary and receive love's healing energy whenever you have need of it.

I was surprised by the symbol I received: it was a see-saw, with myself on one end and the loving person on the other! The main qualities were harmony and balance and the loving energy came in the form of musical sounds. I imagined myself surrounded by those restorative vibrations.

DEALING WITH PHYSICAL PAIN

A young woman came to see me who suffered from severe dysmenorrhoea. This meant that she was often in extreme pain for one or two days during her period and the condition was seriously debilitating. She said that the pain was just beginning to come on now and she was feeling panicky in case she was unable to drive home. I assured her that I would see her safely there if necessary. Having endured this condition myself, I felt deeply sympathetic towards her. She had consulted her doctor, who had prescribed painkillers, but since the condition usually resulted in vomiting, these were quite useless.

I explained to her that the pain was caused largely by contraction of the muscles, so it was important to practise deep physical relaxation. After teaching her this (*see* Introduction), I explained to her that I would lead her through a visualisation that would help to alleviate the condition.

First I asked her to describe the pain to me. She said it was deep in her abdomen and had a dragging sensation, making her feel nauseous and faint. Sometimes it was so bad that she found herself writhing on the floor in agony, in a futile attempt to discover a position that would lessen the cramps. I asked her to think of a symbol that would be illustrative of this. She found this difficult, so I suggested that maybe it had a colour or shape of some kind.

'It's a horrible black-purple, a great messy mass of it, and in the middle something red and heaving, like molten lava.' She hesitated and then said, 'Now I can see myself looking down into the middle of a crater and the lava is red hot and boiling below me.'

'Is the black-purple stuff still there?'

'That seems to have hardened and formed into rock around the crater.'

'How do you feel as you witness this boiling lava below you?'

'Hopeless. This is a terrible thing that I have to endure, over and over again.'

'Is there anything at all that might help you with this horrible situation? Have a look around the landscape and tell me what you see.'

'I see some clouds scudding across the sky and realise that if the wind would blow them my way, then some rain might fall on to the lava and cool it.'

'Then just imagine this happening now. As you watch the clouds, you hear the wind blowing and see them being driven towards you. Now they are directly above you and large drops of rain fall into the crater. Tell me what happens next.'

'As I look down into the crater the lava hisses and sizzles as the raindrops plop on to it. The boiling and bubbling gradually lessens, until it is almost smooth.'

'Watch a little longer.'

'It's quite smooth now and the red colour changes to a grey. The lava is hardening. Now it is pouring with rain and a lake is forming in the crater.'

'How do you feel now?'

'Much calmer. More in control and less hopeless.'

After finishing the visualisation and opening her eyes, I asked my client how bad the pain was. She said it had eased considerably.

This is a condensed example to show how you might invent a fantasy that will help you to cope better with any pain you are suffering. Use the following steps.

Focus on the pain and find adjectives to describe it. See it in terms of colours and shapes, and conjure up a symbol for it. Ask yourself how you feel towards the symbol. Do you wish to express anything towards it? Open up a dialogue if this seems to be appropriate.

Now have a look around and see if there is anything that can help with the difficult situation. Take time to summon up the helpful agent. You may need to request its assistance. What is its response? Allow the scene to unfold in your imagination and witness the helpful being soothing the symbol of your pain. How do you feel now?

After completing the fantasy and opening your eyes, consider whether your pain has eased.

SOOTHING AWAY STRESS

A group of us, all counsellors or psychotherapists, had worked hard one morning looking at important ethical issues. It was time for some light relief, so the facilitator picked up a book of poetry and read from it at random. The poem was about a man and his donkey, how he neglected and beat it, yet still expected it to carry his burdens every day. At the end I found myself bursting into tears. They poured down my cheeks uncontrollably and only with huge difficulty could I stifle some of the sobs. I knew I was with a caring and understanding group of people, so felt no shame for my tears.

Everyone was quietly attentive. The facilitator, a remarkably intuitive person, said gently: 'Is that what you do to yourself?' I nodded. It was true. My Miss Whip subpersonality had been bullying me again, driving me to take on more and more work until I was virtually on my knees with exhaustion. Could I never learn? It was just this same scenario that had finally propelled me into hospital some years ago with a life-threatening illness. Subsequently, with much help from a wise counsellor, I had become skilful at saying 'no' to external demands, and had managed to create a much more relaxed lifestyle for myself, which had been extremely beneficial. Yet secretly Miss Whip had been exerting her influence again, and I had hardly noticed, despite the increasing stress symptoms of racing heart and painful tension in my chest. Obediently, obligingly, my donkey self had submitted to her demands and was now suffering from the scars of her whiplashes and the weight of the huge burdens she strapped on to me. How could I be so cruel to myself?

While these thoughts were racing around my head, the facilitator placed a drawing pad on my knee and a basket full of coloured crayons at my side. She suggested that I close my eyes and visualise the over-burdened animal. Then I had to imagine taking the load off its back, offering it a carrot, and weaving flowers into its mane. Perhaps it might need a way of summoning help when in need, so I pictured him with a bell around his neck which he could reach and ring with his knee. Then I opened my eyes and drew my donkey in a flower-filled meadow, with its ears pricked up, munching his carrot and looking the picture of contentment. I then affirmed to the group that I would have donkey-caring days, during which I would take out my picture and remind myself that self-ministration was top priority for the next twenty-four hours. As I did this, I experienced a glorious lightness and sense of freedom. My heart was no longer racing and the chest tension had eased. I thanked the group members for their warm support and gave each person a fervent hug.

The harmfulness of chronic stress is now common knowledge, with innumerable articles in newspapers and magazines to remind us that it can lead to the killer conditions of heart disease, strokes and cancer. Why is this? Modern life in Western nations demands that we constantly suppress natural reactions in situations that might be perceived as fearful, threatening, frustrating or boring. These may range from on-going fury with the boss for unfair treatment or being stuck in traffic jams, to the pressure of city crowds or the tediousness of repetitive work. It is not appropriate to yell at the boss, ram the car ahead, shove the crowds out of the way, or smash up machinery. If we do, there are likely to be unpleasant consequences! So instead we sit on our anger, swallow down the frustration and boredom, and deny the natural 'flight or fight' response. In this way, long-term stress builds up.

Our hunter-gatherer forebears were not subjected to such frustrations. A threatening situation, such as a rhinoceros charging out of the bush, could be dealt with quickly, either by running away or by defending oneself. The physiological changes that result when the body is put on alert, including increase of the heart rate, blood rushing to the large muscles and brain, the digestive system slowing down, and the pores opening up, are designed to deal with this kind of emergency situation, not the sort that challenges us in modern life. Adrenalin and some thirty other hormones are also released, acting as chemical 'messengers' to various parts of the body. You will be familiar with that rush of adrenalin, but another group of hormones called corticosteroids cannot be sensed in this way, and these have a damaging effect on the immune system. Our bodies are thus in a state of high alert, but no running or fighting follows, so the hormones course around uselessly in the blood stream, the heart thumps and we feel sweaty, but all to no avail. If our bodies are often in this condition, the result to our health can be devastating.

In addition to regular exercise to release the build-up of tension, it is vital to practise deep physical relaxation frequently as described in the Introduction. This double approach will offset the negative physical effects of anxiety and stress. You can also calm yourself by meditating on a peaceful scene. Here are some suggestions.

Inner repose
After relaxing fully allow yourself to meditate on one of the following:

> *a distant landscape of rolling green hills*
> *fluffy white clouds in a blue sky*
> *a quiet harbour with small boats bobbing gently on the water*
> *snow-covered pine trees*
> *a cat curled up by a log fire*
> *listening to soothing music by candlelight*
> *a moonlit garden*

Whichever scene you choose, take time to capture fully its peacefulness. Breathe in the quality of repose and allow it to pervade your whole being. Stay with this feeling and when you open your eyes bring it with you into your daily life.

If you practise relaxation and meditation three times a day, you will find your overall stress levels dropping considerably. Remember that if you are short of time, you can substitute the quick relaxation technique. You can also practise the above meditations at odd moments, while queuing in the supermarket, sitting in a train, or waiting for the kettle to boil. Become accustomed to that inner repose until it feels natural to you.

Internal conflict

The sort of stress I was suffering from was largely the result of an internal conflict in which one part of my personality was putting undue pressure on another part. You may have discovered a similar process in yourself when getting to know your subpersonalities (*see* Chapter 1). Do you sense that this is happening now? If so, then become fully aware of it, as follows.

The arbitrator
Listen carefully to whatever you are telling yourself and make some notes. What part of you is this and what exactly do you say? Is there another aspect of yourself that responds either obligingly, stubbornly or angrily perhaps? When you have a sense of what the internal conflict is about, open up

*the dialogue and write it down, using your imagination to
fill it out as appropriate.*

*Close your eyes and visualise who within you is saying
these things, evoking first the aggressor and then the victim.
See the facial expression, body posture and so on of each,
whether a person or animal.*

*When clear subpersonalities have formed, make
drawings of them. Now set out three chairs in the room
facing inwards, and place the drawings on two of them.
Pick up one illustration and sit in that seat, assuming the
subpersonality, and speak to the character opposite. (For
example my Miss Whip would be frowning and
complaining: 'Hurry up and get on with that work. You're
dawdling as usual . . .', and Donkey would apologise:
'Sorry, I'm day-dreaming again. I know I'm stupid . . .')
Now sit in the other seat, take up the posture and
expression of that subpersonality and make the reply.
Continue until you are clear what the argument is about.*

*Now stand up and give yourself a shake and a stretch.
Step away from both these subpersonalities and sit in the
third seat. You are now in the position of objective observer
and are going to arbitrate between the two contenders. Take
time to appreciate their differences and the nature of their
conflict. Give them some impartial advice. Does one of them
need more time and attention?*

*Write down what happened and how you should
proceed in future in order to reduce the internal stress.*

Awareness of what is happening in your psyche gives you
the option of doing something to change the dynamic.
Remember, this is not about trying to get rid of a subpersonality, but rather appreciating what each has to offer.

The other type of stress is caused by external factors over which one has little control, such as the death of someone close or redundancy at work. The ways in which we respond to and cope with stress are crucial. If overwhelming feelings such as grief or anger are the problem, then you will find some help with these in the next chapter.

If we perceive our situation to be hopeless, feeling stuck or trapped, and that whatever we do will make no difference, then this is cause for very serious concern and professional help must be sought. Research has shown that such people are more likely to succumb to serious illness.

A symbol for a symptom

Another way to help yourself by using your imagination is to focus fully on whatever stress symptom is bothering you and then call to mind a symbol that represents it. You can then create a fantasy that will ameliorate the situation or resolve the problem in a symbolic way. The body responds directly to imagery, much more so than to words, so after working in this way you will find that the symptom has reduced in intensity or even disappeared altogether. The power of the imagination is truly amazing! To give you a clearer idea of what to do, I will describe a real-life example.

One day I received a letter from a friend saying that her neighbour, whose name was David, was in a bad way. Could he call me for advice? When he telephoned a few days later, he had difficulty in speaking, perhaps being unused to expressing his feelings or owning up to any kind of weakness. His firm had apparently been undergoing a 'rationalisation' process; several people had lost their jobs and others, including David, had been demoted. Not only did this mean less interesting work, but also a reduced salary, which, with a new baby on the way, was a serious worry. He had therefore taken on an extra part-time evening job in a pub to make up the difference in income, with the result that he felt perpetually exhausted and stressed and was complaining of chest pains. His doctor had checked his blood pressure, which was fine, and then prescribed tranquillisers, but they made him feel dozy and less able to endure each day. What should he do? I suggested that he should come and see me right away.

He arrived looking haggard. There were deep shadows under his eyes and his breathing was shallow and wheezy. First I taught him how to do the deep relaxation exercise (described in the Introduction). Then I asked him to close his eyes and tell me what the chest pains were like.

'There's a kind of constriction inside me,' he said. 'Something seems to be weighing down on me, causing pressure.'

'Can you say what this thing is like that is weighing down on you?'

He hesitated. 'Something very heavy. Yes, very heavy to cause such a pressure.'

'Can you get an image for this heavy thing – just whatever first comes to mind.'

'Bricks. It's like a pile of bricks. I can almost see them piled up on my chest in a sort of pyramid shape.'

'It sounds extremely painful. Can you see anyone nearby who could help you at all?'

After a pause, David said, 'A colleague from work. I don't know why I should suddenly think of him, but he's very laid-back. Always ready to have a joke.'

'How about asking him to take the bricks off your chest? Imagine doing that and see what happens.'

'OK. Yes, he picks up the top one.'

'How does that feel?'

'A little easier.'

'Now request that he take off the others.'

'He removes the next two, then the layer of three. Phew, just a few more to go!'

At this juncture, I noticed that David's breathing was becoming easier. 'Imagine him taking off the remainder.'

'This is more difficult. Yes, I can see him doing it.'

'Good. How is your chest now?'

'Much freer.'

'Take a few deep, slow breaths, opening up your chest fully.'

When David had completed the exercise I asked him about the pains. He admitted, in astonishment, that they had completely disappeared. I warned him that they might return since the cause of the stress still remained, but if so he could keep them at bay by repeating the visualisation and practising deep relaxation.

The imaginary appearance of his colleague had also seemed significant. Was this perhaps suggesting that those carefree, humorous qualities were the very ones that David himself was not allowing into his life? David immediately saw the truth in this and we subsequently looked at how he might express the fun side of his personality.

Now it is your turn.

*Focus on the symptom that is bothering you, be fully aware
of the type of sensation involved, and call to mind an image
for it. Picture a helpful being nearby. This might be
someone you know, or it could be a subpersonality you have
met, or maybe some sort of animal. Ask for assistance,
making specific requests. See what happens. Be aware that
the symptom is becoming less troublesome. Continue the
visualisation until the problem is resolved.*

*When you open your eyes, check whether the symptom
has actually lessened and write about this experience.*

The hurt part

Many aches, pains and other disorders have a psychosomatic element. In other words, your emotional state has
affected your body in some way and disease has resulted.
Very often these are disorders that your doctor cannot
help you with. If this is the case and you need to find out
more about what is happening within your body, then
use your imagination to go right down inside yourself.
Have faith that your intuition will tell you what you need
to know.

*After settling yourself in an easy chair, pay attention to the
part of you that hurts or is suffering from some kind of
disorder. Be fully aware of the type of discomfort involved.
What exactly is it like? Think of some adjectives to describe
it.*

*Now see yourself in your mind's eye. You are going on
a journey down into your body to the hurt part, but first of
all you must become very, very small. Watch yourself as
you reduce in size until you are tiny.*

You walk down a long flight of steps until you eventually see yourself inside a cavern, which has a stream running through it. You are on a landing stage and tied to it is a miniature boat. You step into it and float away towards the part that needs inspection. Allow yourself to experience this journey and note what happens on the way.

When you arrive at your destination, tie the boat up and give yourself plenty of time to make your investigation. What is this place like? How do you feel here? What has gone wrong? See your disorder in symbolic form. What does it need to make it better? Ask it! If a figure appears, then hold a conversation with it. Find out as much as you can. When you have all the information you need, promise that you will help with the healing and that you will supply the hurt part with whatever it needs.

When your investigation is complete, make your return journey in the boat. Tie it by the landing stage and climb up the steps until you are once more in the world. Watch as you grow back to your normal size.

Open your eyes, write about your journey and in particular make a plan for self-healing. Recall what it is that your hurt part needs and make a commitment to supply it.

A model of yourself

When I was recovering from cancer, my therapist suggested that it might be helpful for me to become more aware of my relationship with my body and learn about the messages that my illness had been sending me. He then gave me some plasticine and instructed me to close my eyes and make a model of myself, using touch only.

This was a challenging exercise. First of all I modelled my head, using plenty of plasticine for the hair, and making sure that my nose turned up at the tip. These were features that I liked. The arms and legs were muscular and strong, and I paid particular attention to the fingers. The torso, however, was a real problem, especially the area around the chest. I felt uneasy about modelling my breasts, especially the one that had been damaged by cancer.

When I opened my eyes and saw the resulting figure, I hardly knew whether to laugh or cry, but I realised at once that it represented the internal body image that I carried of myself. In the discussion that followed I discovered that I used my long hair to hide behind and felt peculiarly unsafe if I wore it up or swept away from my face. My carefully modelled hands were expressive of my musicality, my strong legs my love of dancing. The difficulty around the chest area had to do with ambivalent feelings towards my femininity, and it became obvious that this was the subject that needed the most urgent treatment.

My counsellor pointed out that I had spent many years in a highly competitive business environment, expressing the more masculine aspects of my character. My illness seemed to be suggesting that the feminine side had been neglected. I knew he was right. For a long time now I had felt out of balance with myself, without understanding what this meant. How could I correct this and allow my feminine energies free rein? My counsellor asked me what the breast symbolised to me, and I replied that it had to do with caring and nurturing. So the message was clear: I had to find a way of bringing these loving qualities into my life to a far greater extent than hitherto. It was largely this piece of work that inspired me to make the commitment to train as a therapist myself, work which I find deeply rewarding.

If you are suffering from some form of illness, try and discover the hidden messages by making a model of yourself. You may like to ask a trusted friend or family member to help facilitate this process.

You will need clay or plasticine, a board to work on, and a long, soft scarf. Ask your friend to blindfold you. Now take a while to meditate on your body and be particularly aware of any vulnerable parts. When you feel ready, make a model of yourself using touch only. Note any feelings and thoughts that occur to you during this process.

When it is finished ask your friend to remove the blindfold. Try not to be critical of your model – there is no right way to make it! Discuss together what your figure tells you about yourself and any feelings that it evokes in you. Do you have any insights into what your illness symbolises? What are the hidden messages?

In the light of this new information, what direction should you now take? Make an action plan, beginning with the simplest step.

GIVING UP SMOKING

Having climbed the few stairs to my consulting room, Bill was red-faced and breathing heavily. He was clearly very out of condition. Moreover, I could smell the tobacco fumes on his clothes and had a sudden urge to open the window. How could I help? He confessed that he had tried to give up smoking, but without success, despite his doctor's dire warnings about the state of his health. I explained that a combination of counselling with visualisation had proved very useful in other cases, but that ultimately he was the person who had to give up the smoking; I couldn't do it for him!

After describing the sort of damage that long-term smoking inflicts on the air passages, I suggested that he might like to use his imagination to have a look around his lungs. If he could see the state they were in, that might motivate him to cut down. He groaned at the thought of this, but said he was willing to give it a try.

A tour of the lungs

After persuading Bill to relax and making sure that he felt comfortable with his eyes closed, I asked him to describe to me how his lungs felt. He said they were tight and wheezy. I told him that he was going to parachute down into his lungs, but first of all he must imagine becoming small enough to do this.

'Can you see yourself as a miniature parachutist?'

After a while he nodded.

'The journey you are about to take may be hazardous, so you will need some kind of lucky charm or talisman to keep you safe. What could that be?'

'I don't know why I've suddenly thought of this, but it's a blue necklace that my mother used to wear. I loved it as a small kid because it sparkled. I'll put that in my pocket.'

'Fine. Now imagine that you are taking a jump into a deep shaft, and the parachute supports you as you sail gently downwards. Have a look around and tell me what that's like.'

'It's rather dark and I feel apprehensive. I'm going down quite slowly, but jerkily as the breath goes in and out. It's a sort of dark-red tube. It smells horrible. There are little things protruding from the sides, struggling to move, but they are trapped in black sticky stuff.'

'What do they want?'

'To be free so that they can move again.'

'What do they need, to achieve this?'

'Fresh air. There isn't much of that down here.'

'How about making a commitment to giving them that?'

He nods. 'OK.'

'Keep going.'

'I can see the tube dividing into two, but I'm not sure whether to go right or left, so I land on the island between them. Then I jump down the right one. Now there are lots of different passageways all getting narrower and narrower. It's very confusing. It's difficult to breathe and I feel claustrophobic. There's a sort of rattling noise. Now I've landed and I'm sinking into thick, slimy mud. The parachute has got entangled and I don't know how I'm going to get out.'

At this point I needed to check that Bill was all right: 'Remember that you can open your eyes if you need to.'

'No. I'm OK, but it's really nasty down here. I have a strong feeling that I don't want to die.'

'So how can you best survive? In this imaginary world anything is possible. Perhaps the necklace can help you.'

'The landscape is changing. There's a tree branch above me. I realise that I can loop the necklace over it and hang on to it so that I don't sink down any further. Smoke starts to billow around me and I can hear my mother's voice saying, "You always were good at creating smoke-screens". I'm not sure what she means by that. Now one of those cherubs with puffed-out cheeks appears. I feel more hopeful.'

'Would you like to make a request of it?'

'Yes. "For goodness' sake get me out of this mess." "Only if you stop polluting us", it says. Now I don't know what to reply because I don't think I can stop.'

'How do you feel towards it?' I ask.

'Guilty. I know I shouldn't do this.'

'So what's your reason for creating these smoke-screens?' I ask.

'So no one can see me, I guess,' he said thoughtfully. 'I don't feel like a very nice person to know.'

'Tell it.' At this point Bill has a dialogue with the cherub. He discovers that, to help him give up smoking, he needs to build up his feelings of self-worth. He promises to do that, and in return the cherub blows warm air at the mud until it turns to sand. He frees the parachute and Bill is able to float back up to the world and return to his normal size.

When Bill opened his eyes, he was staggered at the insight revealed in this fantasy. He admitted that he had always been very shy and that he found personal relationships difficult. He decided to continue with counselling to build up his confidence, and meanwhile would gradually cut back on the cigarettes with my support.

If you wish to give up smoking, investigation of your lungs may help you too. Remember to take a talisman with you.

Become a miniature parachutist and float down your windpipe. What is it like in here? What do your lungs need from you? Do you meet any creatures? If so, strike up a conversation and try to discover your reasons for this addiction. What do you need to assist you with this problem? Can your talisman help you in any way?

When you have completed the visualisation, float back into the world and return to your normal size. Make a commitment to yourself, starting with the easiest step.

Readers who experience breathing difficulties caused or worsened by psychological factors may like to adapt the above visualisation to gain further insight into the problem.

HEALTHY EATING

If you suffer from any kind of eating disorder, it is essential that you seek professional guidance. Food is deeply symbolic and has many emotional associations. You will therefore need sympathetic support if you want to come to terms with what is happening inside you.

Many people who overeat say that the layers of fat give them some form of protection. Some admit that stuffing the food down themselves, even if their bodies don't want it, helps to suppress strong feelings. Others describe the hollow inside themselves that no amount of food seems to fill. The questions that arise here are: how can protection be given, strong feelings safely dealt with, or the need for love fulfilled without resorting to more food than the body really needs? Bulimics may not have learned how to receive warmth and nourishment from others, or may not trust it when offered, so it has to be spewed out. There may also be sexual connotations, such as the anorexic girl who does not allow her body to fill out into womanhood.

This subject is too complex to be dealt with in any great detail here but useful insights may be gained by making notes in your diary or workbook concerning your eating habits and seeing if any patterns emerge. What are the triggers that set off the symptoms of your disorder? Are there any hints as to what the food represents for you?

Also consider joining a self-help group. Other people can be a great encouragement and you will know then that you are not alone with your difficulty.

The temple of your soul

In the desperate effort to use food to fulfil deep psychological and emotional needs, we very often find ourselves out of touch with our bodies' true physical requirements for optimum functioning. Make it your business to learn about healthy eating and develop a plan that is right for your particular physique.

Before a meal, focus on your body and tune in to what its physiological requirements are. Does it need less food just now, or more? What kind of nutrients, how much and how often would be ideal for it? If you have a weight problem, create a vision of yourself as just the right size for your build.

Imagine yourself eating healthy fruit and vegetables, and see the good that they do as their nutrients enter your bloodstream. Feel that spurt of energy, see your shining hair and clear skin. Be in awe of the amazingly complex processes that keep you alive. How can you best support these?

Adopt an attitude of respect for your body. Remind yourself that this is the temple of your soul and you are its caretaker. This is a responsible job, one that deserves to be carried out with love. See yourself nurturing your temple with loving care.

Repeat this visualisation often.

PHYSICAL EXERCISE

We frequently hear that we must do some sort of exercise in order to remain healthy, but how easy it is to make those excuses! Oh, I'm too tired, too busy, or I just don't feel like it today. Visualisation not only ensures that exercise is beneficial, it can also help with motivation and make it more fun.

Animal images
Whatever form of exercise you choose, find an animal image for it. For example, if you have taken up running, then picture yourself as a graceful gazelle bounding light-footed across grassland. You will be surprised how this helps to banish tiredness!

Swimmers may choose to imagine themselves as frogs, completely at home in the water, with strong legs that propel them forward with speed. They will find themselves accomplishing those extra lengths with unex-pected ease.

Now conjure up your own animal image. Make a drawing or cut out a picture of it and hang it on a wall where you will see it frequently. As part of your preparation for the exercise, meditate on the animal and adopt its spirit.

AT EASE WITH SEXUALITY

Late one evening when relaxing by the fire and contemplating my future, I found myself in the midst of the following reverie.

'I am in a circus tent, sitting in the audience. The arena is dark except for a red spotlight which shines on two acrobats, a young man and a woman, both with superb physiques. Their act is skilfully sensual as their bodies intertwine, performing graceful balances, tumbles and throws. The shapes they create together are both erotic and aesthetically beautiful.

'After a while the act progresses to a trapeze, and the girl flies across the wide space under the canopy, letting go of one bar to grab another with perfect timing. They perform daring somersaults, catching each other then executing holds that require extraordinary strength. These two people are vibrantly alive, celebrating the exquisiteness of the human body.

'Now in my imagination I become the female acrobat. My sequinned leotard and soft ballet shoes allow complete freedom of movement and I revel in the beautiful patterns and shapes that my body can make. I am in touch with my sexual energy and enjoy contact with the man as we perform the tumbles and throws together. Between us there is absolute trust.

'Up on the trapeze there is a tremendous sense of exhilaration as I fly across the open space. I feel totally in tune with the rhythm of the swings and it is this, combined with the focus, that enables me to have such perfect timing. My body alternates between calm relaxation and tautness, depending on the move involved. As the blood pulsates through my veins I rejoice in my vitality. I am strongly aware of my sexuality as a source of creative energy. My promise to myself is to take that with me into the world.'

This was the imagery that occurred to me quite spontaneously when considering what I needed in order to move forward on my path. The sensuality was unexpected, but I was already feeling marvellously alive, having just met my present husband! The visualisation helped me to appreciate that my new-found radiance could be expressed not just privately, but also creatively in the outside world. This was a vision of sexuality as a source of energy that could be directed at will.

Sadly, the technological world of the West seems to view sexuality as a mechanical function. We no longer talk about making love, with the emotional involvement and sensuality that the phrase implies, but rather about 'having sex', as if it were a cup of tea or a sandwich. Making love with someone we care deeply about can be the most rewarding and life-enhancing of all human experiences, yet so often guilt and fear get in the way, preventing us from celebrating our bodies in this most natural way.

If you wish to tap into your sexuality, begin by recalling a time when your body felt most alive, at its most sensual. Re-

*experience those sensations in your imagination and allow
an image to form. Then let the fantasy unfold, noticing the
qualities that present themselves and the energy involved.*

*Step into the part of the protagonist. If several
characters have appeared, choose the one with whom you
most closely identify. What is that like? How do you feel?*

*Does any transformation need to take place? If so,
what or who might help you with that? What happens next?*

*What kind of energy do you now experience and what
do you wish to do with it? Is there any message for you here,
any insight? What is your next step in relation to your
sexuality?*

Chapter 4
Happier Relationships

Giving love and appreciation.
Standing in someone else's shoes.
Being a good friend. Coping with powerful feelings.
Dealing with resentments. How to forgive.
Psychological protection. Accepting your parents.
Recovery from bereavement.

The way in which people walk up the stairs leading to my consulting room gives me a clue about their present mood and maybe a brief insight into their character. On this particular occasion, two pairs of feet stamped their way up and I was immediately on the alert, expecting anger. I was right. Erica and Stanley, after flinging their coats on the floor, sat in their chairs in furious silence. I waited expectantly, wondering who would attack first.

At last Erica spoke: 'We've just had a flaming row in the car,' she said.

'Can you explain what that was about?' I asked.

'I'm frustrated, frustrated!' she screamed. 'I'm bored and lonely with the kids at school, and it's impossible to get a decent job around here.' To her husband: 'You just don't appreciate how horrible my life is, especially with you being away so often on business trips. You're never here. Never here to see what our life is like! What's the point of being married? You've never loved me or cared about the kids. I know you haven't. When you're at home, you spend all the time in front of the telly – you might just as well not be there for all the attention you give us. I'm not a nasty person, I know I'm not, but I feel so terrible when we row in front of the kids. We shouldn't do that. But the truth is, I hate you, I hate you!' To me: 'All I want is to be rid of him, but he won't listen, he never listens,' she wailed, and at this point burst into tears.

Her voice was harsh and high-pitched and her mouth pressed into a hard line. Yet she was an attractive and intelligent young woman. Clearly something had gone seriously wrong with this relationship. I handed her a tissue and said, 'You sound very angry, Erica. From what you say, it seems that you feel unappreciated by Stanley, and that when he is at home he doesn't pay you enough attention.' She nodded sullenly and sniffed. Then I turned to Stanley, who had a deep frown on his face. 'Erica has been accusing you of lack of care and attention. Is there some truth in what she says?'

'Probably, yes. I know I should spend more time at home, but when I'm there she nags me, so I switch the telly on to shut her up.'

'What else can I do but nag you, you lazy sod?' she screeched. 'When did you last do the washing up or clean the floor? When, when? Never, that's what, never. Not even when I was ill with glandular fever. I'll never forgive you for that.' To me: 'I was so weak and feverish, yet he did nothing to help me. He wouldn't even bring me a cup of tea. I had to crawl out of bed to try and make some soup to keep myself going. I even had to clean up after the cat had been sick on the floor. I felt so unloved and uncared for,' at which she broke into more sobs. 'How could I possibly do the housework when I was feeling so weak? I remember looking at the pile of washing up in the sink and thinking, is this all there is to life – this mess?'

Stanley shifted uncomfortably in his seat. 'That's true. I was a selfish bastard, but I just didn't really notice it. I didn't leave the mess on purpose.'

The dialogue continued like this for some time, with accusations, counter-accusations or defensiveness. Yet this couple had been married for nine years, so what had kept them together? It transpired that Stanley admired Erica's intelligence, but considered that her frustration was partly due to her inability to stick at things. For example, she had given up her university course. While he admitted to selfishness, he also felt blamed for things that were not his fault. He seemed to be motivated to try and change and improve their relationship, while Erica, having declared that she wanted to be rid of him, seemed unsure of what she really wanted when asked directly. Firstly, she needed to find a way of trusting him and believing that he was genuinely willing to make some adjustments.

RESTORING LOVE

It is a fundamental part of human nature to long for love and attention. If we don't receive that warmth, we shrivel inside. Close personal relationships depend on the giving and receiving of love and they thrive on quality time spent together and on each person feeling fully understood and appreciated by the other. After living with the same partner for a long time, it is so easy to take that person for granted and become deaf to his or her needs. Loving feelings can be renewed by meditating on that individual, reminding yourself of the qualities that you originally found so appealing, and promising yourself that you will tell your partner how much you still appreciate these aspects. Make a pledge to give 100 per cent undivided attention when he or she tells you something or needs your assistance.

Renewed appreciation

Take time from your busy schedule to reflect on the most significant person in your life. Close your eyes and recall your first meeting. When was this and what was the occasion? Who else was there? See the scene once again in your mind's eye. What was your initial impression? What was he or she wearing? Picture the pose, the facial expression. Can you identify the most attractive qualities? How did you feel then?

Now reflect on the intervening years and the time you have spent with this person. Have there been any changes? What do you still admire and like about your partner, either little idiosyncrasies, physical features or personal qualities? When did you last express these positive thoughts and feelings directly? Make a decision to tell your partner within the next twenty-four hours three things that you truly appreciate about him or her.

Now imagine your significant other telling you something or making a request. Picture yourself responding in the way that you normally do. Is it an absent-minded 'Mm,' while your thoughts are really elsewhere? If so, then rerun the episode, this time picturing yourself giving your partner total and undivided attention. You stop whatever you are doing, look him or her in the eyes, and respond warmly to each part of the tale or request and reflect back your understanding. What effect does this have? Make an inner commitment to put this into practice the next time you are together.

If you are not used to active listening, you may need quite a lot of practice before it comes naturally to you. Counsellors learn how to do this in their training. They soon discover that many of their clients have never been fully heard and understood in their lives, leaving them with a deep need for absolute attention. This is a skill well worth cultivating and a wonderful gift to offer to friends and relatives. Remember to reflect back, or paraphrase in your own words, whatever the person has told you, so that they know you have been listening. You will see an example of this in my response to Erica's outburst near the beginning of the chapter.

Evoking empathy

Part of the problem between Erica and Stanley was a failure to stand in the other person's shoes, to see things from that perspective, in other words to empathise. Stanley had not appreciated that offering to help with chores was a signal to Erica of concern and affection. At the same time Erica had not realised how exhausted Stanley was at the end of a long day's work. If she had suggested gently that he put his feet up for ten minutes after arriving home, he might have felt more like doing some jobs for her a little later, knowing that she was tuned in to his present mood.

Sometimes we know intuitively how another person is feeling, especially if we have had a long-standing connection with that individual, and we may then adjust our behaviour accordingly. At other times we are so full of our own feelings and needs that these totally block whatever unspoken messages are coming our way. In order for your intuitive powers to operate effectively, it is essential to be relaxed and open in attitude. You are then much more likely to pick up subliminal clues, putting you in close touch with the other person's true state of mind. Test this out for yourself when you are next in someone else's company. Meanwhile, meditating on the individual will help you to empathise more deeply.

Standing in someone else's shoes

After relaxing and closing your eyes, allow a detailed picture to form of the person with whom you wish to empathise. See the body posture, the features and typical expression, be aware of the energy. Imagine the person performing customary tasks. How are they done? Acknowledge your own feelings when in this person's presence.

Now imagine that you look down at the floor. You see there a pair of slippers or shoes belonging to this friend or relative. Visualise yourself becoming that person and putting on these slippers or shoes. You stand up and move around, taking on the typical posture. What is that like? What sort of burdens are carried? Where in your body do you sense the tensions and anxieties? Alternatively, is the predominant mood quite laid-back and relaxed? What kind of experiences have formed this character?

Imagine that, as this person, you are having a conversation with your real self. What would you like to say? How do you feel? What do you want of your real self? Does anything get in the way of good communication? Would you like to offer a gift? Continue the dialogue, then disengage from the other person. Step out of the borrowed shoes and become yourself again. Do you wish to reply, to give something, maybe, or make a request?

After opening your eyes, jot down some notes in your workbook concerning this experience. What have you learnt about your friend or relative? Can you now empathise more deeply? In the light of this new knowledge, how might you adjust your behaviour so that your relationship is improved?

Did anything get in the way of this exercise, such as intrusive or difficult thoughts or feelings? If so, what can you do about them? If you have stored up any resentments towards the person, then you may need to work through these yourself first (*see* Dealing with Resentments on page 119).

In my consulting room I often see one partner in a relationship complaining about the other's behaviour. When the feelings are examined it is often discovered that the underlying wish is that the other person would be the same as oneself! Erica had moaned at length about Stanley's unreliability and how he was always late whenever they arranged to meet. On the other hand, Stanley argued that Erica was too fussy and controlling. Their disparity in temperament meant that each had a different relationship to time: to Erica, a given appointment meant that hour precisely, while for Stanley it automatically incorporated an extra five or ten minutes either way. The point is, it is crucial to understand that your partner is different from you. If you wish to live happily together, then you must accept those dissimilarities.

Appreciating another person's differences
Repeat the above meditation, but this time, after putting on the other person's slippers or shoes, focus on all the ways in which he or she is not the same as yourself. Try to understand, from the inside, what causes these dissimilarities. Note and appreciate the advantages in behaving in these other ways.

After reverting to your own identity and before opening your eyes, affirm to yourself: 'I see that — is not the same as myself. Neither of us is right or wrong; we are just different from each other. I accept —'s differences.

Allowing your partner to be their own natural self will ease innumerable little niggles and irritations.

BEING A GOOD FRIEND

In addition to active listening, reflecting back what you have heard, being empathetic and valuing the other person's differences, disclosing your own feelings and experiences to the person you are with offers him or her the opportunity to do the same. This can be very difficult for people who are naturally shy or reserved. It can also be tough for men, because it is not part of the macho culture to express feelings, and they run the risk of the accusation of being a 'wimp'. Imaginary rehearsal can assist with overcoming such inhibitions.

Trevor's job was in an engineering firm, and although he got along with workmates well enough on the surface, he was aware that he lacked meaningful relationships. He had lived with his mother until four years ago, when she had died of cancer. Since then he had been on his own. He felt awkward about going to the pub by himself, feeling nervous about striking up a conversation with a stranger and not knowing what to say. His best moments were going biking with the motorcycle club, but meetings were held only once a month.

It was obvious that Trevor was lacking in confidence, so I suggested that we first of all work with affirmations by considering what his best qualities were as a friend. Here is the list he came up with: 'one of the lads', can chat about men's things, likes a joke and a laugh, interested in people and would like to understand them better. This was a good start. He agreed that the next time he went to the pub, he would put this list in his pocket to boost his confidence. He considered that having an imaginary trial run would be helpful, so he settled into the chair and closed his eyes. This was our conversation:

'So you are about to go down to the local. What are your feelings?' I asked.

'Not sure if I really want to go. I can see myself walking into the pub and not knowing anyone, then feeling really awkward. People turn and look at me. I wish the ground would swallow me up.'

'That sounds really painful. But on this occasion you have your list of affirmations with you and I remember that you are very interested in people. You are also good at talking about men's things and like a good joke. Rerun the scene in your imagination, reminding yourself of your good qualities as a friend. This time put the focus of attention on the people around you rather than on yourself. Who are the people at the bar? Is there anyone sitting on their own who might appreciate someone to talk to? You are a good friend and have much to offer others.'

'OK. Well this time when I go into the pub there's a man sitting on his own in the corner. I've seen him there before and I am curious about him. I give him a nod, buy a pint, then go over to him . . . but I don't know what to say.'

'For now just improvise. This is only an imaginary exercise, so you don't have to get it right.'

'Well, I could say something like "Mind if I join you?" Then maybe ask him if he's local.'

'Excellent! How do you imagine he responds?'

'He seems quite pleased and pulls out a chair for me. Then maybe we chat about what's going on in the town. Now I'm stuck.'

'Check in with your thoughts and feelings. What are they exactly?'

'It's difficult starting up a conversation with a stranger. I'm feeling awkward again.'

'Can you share any of that with him? Perhaps he feels the same way.'

'I hadn't thought of that. Maybe I could say that even though I've lived here some time, people tend to keep themselves to themselves and are difficult to get to know. Then ask if his experience is the same.'

'Good idea. How does he respond this time?'

'He seems to open up a bit and agrees. Then admits that he's not much of a conversationalist.'

'How do you feel towards him now?'

'Well, we have something in common, so I feel easier with him.'

'Of course. So what happens next?'

'I would like to know him better, but am hesitant about asking him questions in case he thinks I'm being too nosy.'

'Well, you could maybe include some of that too and start off with: "I hope you don't think I'm being too nosy . . ." or "Tell me if I'm being too nosy . . .".'

'Yes. I'll do that.'

This imaginary rehearsal continued in a similar vein for some time until Trevor felt much more positive about making friends with strangers. With practice, he realised that being honest about thoughts and feelings moment by moment can ease social relationships and put them on to a more meaningful level. Whenever he felt stuck he would check in with himself and find something suitable to reveal to the other person. This way he was able to overcome his shyness and loneliness and make some new friends.

This, then, is the process whereby you can become a good friend:

Make a list affirming your most friendly qualities.

Think of someone you would like to know better and imagine arranging a meeting. You have your list of affirmations in your pocket.

Evoke the situation and be aware of your thoughts and feelings.

Start up the conversation with this person, putting the attention on that individual.

Empathise, listen attentively and reflect back what you hear.

Find out as much as you can, without being too intrusive.

If you become stuck, check in with your thoughts and feelings and be willing to disclose what they are. What is the response?

At what point does this conversation become more than just casual chat?

How do you feel now?

Be willing to take the risk of putting this into practice.

COPING WITH POWERFUL FEELINGS

If, like Erica, you have allowed resentments to build up over a long period of time, then feelings of anger and hatred could have reached boiling point. Although such feelings may have been triggered by someone else, they are yours and yours alone, so it is important that you adopt a safe way of dealing with them. Finding an image for a powerful emotion can help to relieve it. The following illustration, based on my work with another young woman, demonstrates the process.

Gill was a bundle of nervous energy. She wore a bright red mohair jumper, so vivid that the colour reflected on to her face. She expressed her thoughts and feelings with such force and rapidity that it was tricky to find any gaps in which I could respond. She described in great detail her alcoholic father, her terror of him during childhood, and her feelings of helplessness on the occasions when he attacked her mother, both verbally and physically. The feelings of anger and hatred towards him were still powerfully present, even though she had had little contact with him since leaving home. How could she come to terms with her childhood? How could she deal safely with these overwhelming feelings?

Gradually the eruption abated, and the moment seemed right to suggest a visualisation.

The pressure-cooker

After taking Gill through the deep relaxation exercise (as described in the Introduction), I checked that she felt happy to close her eyes. Then I asked her to focus on the feelings which so disturbed her and to describe them to me. Whereabouts in her body did she experience them?

'They're very intense. They seem to be pushing all the time to get out, pushing against my ribs, which can only just contain them. I can feel their force,' she said, pressing both hands over her diaphragm, as if in an effort to keep them in.

'How would you describe their temperature?' I enquired. 'Hot or cold?'

'Oh, hot,' she replied quickly, 'very, very hot – intensely so.'

'Almost at boiling point?'

'Yes, definitely.'

'Do they have any particular colour?'

'White, white hot, even hotter than red.'

'Does this white heat have any shape at all?'

'It seems to be compressed, squeezed into a small space.'

'Is this forming into a recognisable image?'

'I can see bubbles on the surface of boiling liquid, and white steam forcing its way through a tiny aperture with a hissing sound. Yes, that's it — it's a pressure-cooker. My mother used to have one. I was always frightened of it in case it exploded.'

'And perhaps you're scared that you might explode with the force of your feelings.'

'Yes, sometimes they do seem that bad.'

'So what could you do now with this pressure-cooker to reduce the intensity?'

'I could take the weights off the valve so that more steam could escape.'

'Yes, indeed. Imagine doing that now.' She nods. 'What happens?'

'The steam rushes through the aperture and the force inside the cooker diminishes. The bubbles are not so frantic either.'

'Shift your focus back to your body. Do you notice any changes?'

'There's less pressure against my ribs. My breathing feels easier too,' she said, drawing in the air slowly.

'How about the safety valve? Will that open up if the pressure gets too much again?'

'Oh, yes. I'd forgotten about that.'

'Have a look and make sure it's working OK.'

We continued the visualisation until Gill felt very much better. I then encouraged her to make a drawing of her pressure-cooker. After this session she experienced a wonderful sense of relief.

When we next met, we looked at how she could safely let out steam in relation to her father. She pretended he was sitting with us in the room and she told him in no uncertain terms what she thought of him. In an effort to understand what it was that had driven him to become an alcoholic, she would make time to find out more about his background. Her aunt would be a useful source of information and she resolved to arrange a meeting as soon as possible.

If, like Gill, you are suffering from overwhelming negative feelings, then the image of a pressure-cooker may well be suitable for you, too. On the other hand you may prefer to allow your own image to surface, in which case use the following steps.

Relax and close your eyes. Take some deep breaths.

Tune in to your strong feeling. Be fully aware of its nature. Find adjectives to describe it.

Can you sense it in your body? If so, where exactly?

Does it have a colour or a shape?

Allow an image to form – whatever occurs to you first. Examine it closely.

What does this image most need to do? Does it need help from you or anyone else? Have a look around in your imagination for that assistance. Create a dialogue, if appropriate.

See what happens. Is the strong feeling safely discharged?

Experience the relief.

When you feel ready, bring the visualisation to a satisfying conclusion.

Open your eyes and make a drawing of the symbol.

If you do not feel confident about working with the image on your own, then as soon as you receive it, open your eyes and make a drawing or painting. The process of doing this is likely to be a relief in itself.

This technique can also be applied to a strong positive feeling, such as being so madly in love that your concentration is shot to pieces! After performing the visualisation and doing the drawing, you will be able to focus on work again.

It is crucial to find a safe way of expressing your strong negative feelings. Otherwise they may come out in a way that you do not wish, and you will end up shouting at someone, or worse. Some of my clients have written about their emotions in either prose or poetry or in the form of a letter. Others have had a good yell when there was no one around to hear, or they have beaten up a pillow or cushion or played a hard game of squash. Choose whatever is most appropriate for you, making sure that no one, including yourself, will come to harm. You will then discover that you can deal with the offending person or situation in a much more rational and effective manner.

What's the weather?

The weather is profoundly evocative of mood and has been employed by a great many writers and film directors to set a scene and create atmosphere. You can use it as a metaphor for a prevailing frame of mind, whatever that may be. If you are feeling depressed, you may see an overcast grey sky, or heavy black clouds over a bleak landscape; sadness may be expressed as falling rain.

You can also use this exercise to bring fully to

consciousness the effect that another person has on you. For example, if you experience someone as being too smothering or suffocating towards you, then your image may be of oppressive, humid weather in a tropical setting. Do you get the idea? Use this visualisation if any feeling or mood is troublesome, either your own, or someone else's.

Find a quiet place in which you can relax, then turn your attention to this bothersome mood.

What kind of weather would represent this feeling? Allow a picture of the sky and the landscape to form in your mind's eye.

When you have filled in the details in your imagination, open your eyes and paint or draw your weather picture. How do you feel now? Do you want to make any additions or alterations?

When it is finished, check how much your mood has been alleviated. If your picture represents another person, what have you learnt?

DEALING WITH RESENTMENTS

Is there anyone in your life at the moment towards whom you feel resentful? If so, this usually indicates that you want something from this person, but your need has not been fulfilled.

The question that now arises is: does the person actually know what it is that you want? All too often we expect someone else to be able to read our minds, to know what we require instinctively. This is a remnant of our experiences as babies, when we were dependent on our mothers to know intuitively when we needed to be fed, changed, and so on. If we were lucky, our mother's instinct gave her the right guidance. However, as adults our partners are not our parents! It is unfair to expect them to receive our unspoken messages and interpret them correctly every time. If there is something you want, then make it absolutely explicit by asking for it. This way you avoid any unnecessary build-up of resentments.

Lesley and Melissa had a very loving gay partnership, but they disliked the way they squabbled in the kitchen. Invariably this was about the cooking. Lesley was the sort of person who became so involved in her own activities that she was totally oblivious of something as mundane as food. Amazingly, she rarely suffered from hunger, whereas her partner did. As Melissa's blood sugar dropped, her temper became shorter and Lesley became the target of her grumpiness. She would end up cooking the dinner in a bad mood, never saying what her true feelings were. Petty arguments were then the inevitable result.

When we enquired into what it was that Melissa wanted, it was quite simply that Lesley should take on more domestic responsibility. After having cooked the dinner for three nights in a row, she began to feel resentful that Lesley was not doing her share. Yet she had felt diffident about making a straightforward request. Lesley meanwhile had been mystified by the bad moods. After becoming accustomed to asking for what she wanted, and discovering that her partner responded warmly, Melissa found that the irritations vanished and peace was restored in the kitchen.

If resentments are your problem, the following visualisation should help to put you on the right track.

I want you to ...
Find a quiet place and allow yourself to connect with your feelings of resentment. Call to mind the person who has apparently caused these feelings. Imagine that you are telling the individual why you are so angry, making simple statements, each one beginning, 'I resent you for ...' Picture the response.

Now consider the things you like and appreciate about the person, however small they may be. Imagine telling him or her these things, again using straightforward statements, this time beginning, 'I appreciate you for ...' What is the response this time?

Focus again on your feelings and try to discover what it is that you want from the person that hasn't been supplied. Allow the need or needs to become clear. Now you are going to imagine making requests. First, decide on the best timing, when the person is most likely to be responsive. Your statements will begin, 'I want you to ...' See yourself asking for whatever you require. Picture your need being fulfilled. Thank the person. Create a vision of your relationship improving.

How do you feel now? Promise yourself that you will make requests rather than permit an accumulation of resentments.

It is up to you to carry this out in real life.

FORGIVENESS

Feeling very angry with someone over a long period can erode your own happiness and can even have a detrimental effect on your health. It is much better, therefore, to find a way of forgiving that person and moving on. However, there is a right time for forgiveness, and it is usually only possible after your anger has been dealt with and any unfulfilled need met in some other way.

Mary was in her early forties with a flare for unusual clothes and jewellery that set off her dark hair and strong features. She wore a handcrafted silver torque round her neck and, as she spoke, she fingered the large amber pendant suspended from it. Knowing nothing of its significance, I admired the beauty of the stone. Suddenly she began to sob. After recovering herself a little she explained that the necklace had been a gift from Geoffrey, the man in her life. They had lived together for six years, but eighteen months ago she had been devastated to discover that he had secretly been seeing another woman. Moreover, Mary had been paying money into a joint account for house improvements. While believing that Geoffrey had been away on a business trip, he had in fact almost emptied their account and spent the proceeds on a luxury break in Paris with this younger woman. This double betrayal had been terrible; her trust had been totally violated. So far she had been unable to accept him back into her life, despite the fact that the affair was over. He had confessed his guilt, and promised that such a thing would never happen again, but Mary's feelings of anger and jealousy were still raw. How could she find a way of coping with them? How could she ever forgive him?

I explained that forgiveness was indeed possible, but first she must find a safe strategy for discharging her strong feelings. She admitted that she had never really told Geoffrey what emotional agony he had inflicted on her, so she decided to pour out her thoughts and feelings in a letter to him, one that she would not send. She would post him a revised version at a later date. She also worked with the visualisation recommended for dealing with strong negative feelings.

After recalling how she had nearly fainted when first hearing about her partner's secret affair, she saw an image of herself walking along the edge of a precipice and being overwhelmed with a fear of falling as she looked down into the abyss below. As we investigated this image, we realised that extreme insecurity and dread of abandonment lay beneath the jealousy. Mary was puzzled by this because she had always felt loved and valued by her parents. However, when we probed deeper she spontaneously recalled an occasion during her childhood when her mother was acutely ill with peritonitis and was rushed into hospital. There had been no time to prepare Mary for this event and she had been overcome with terror that her mother would die and that she would never see her again. She remembered being inconsolable with fear and grief.

Mary was amazed that this one event could have had such a long-lasting effect, but it seemed that, ever since that date, she had felt that no one, however well-intentioned, could ever be 100 per cent reliable. To guard against future hurt, therefore, she gradually learned to be strong and independent. I explained that the little girl who had felt so desperately insecure still resided in her. However, she herself could find ways to comfort and protect this inner child through visualisation and drawing. First, I asked her to close her eyes and conjure up an image of herself at the time of her mother's hospitalisation. She saw five-year-old Mary sitting cross-legged on the floor in a checked dress and pigtails, her hands over her eyes and tears streaming down her face. Then she made a drawing of the image.

'What does this little girl most need?' I asked.

'Hugs and reassurance,' came the response. So Mary visualised the small child receiving these from her mother. She then made a second drawing of the girl being hugged. This time there was a huge beam on her face. I recommended to Mary that she put this up on the wall at home to remind herself to give this comfort to her own inner child on a regular basis.

The moment in therapy had now arrived whereby we could explore, very gently, the ways in which Mary, albeit unwittingly, might have helped to set the scene leading to Geoffrey's behaviour. He must have known that their joint bank statement showing the missing money would immediately alert her. It was almost as if Geoffrey had wanted to be found out. So was there some unconscious message here? She admitted that her super-independence might sometimes make her appear aloof, and she had been rather too deeply involved in her work. Perhaps Geoffrey had felt neglected and was making a huge bid for attention.

We decided to test out this hypothesis with a Gestalt exercise, and Mary imagined that Geoffrey was sitting in the empty chair facing her. She saw him leaning forward towards her and the expression in his eyes seemed to be pleading. When she asked him what he needed from her, he immediately replied, 'Your time.' Mary apologised for appearing remote and promised to give him the full attention that he wanted. In return, what could he give her? She requested renewed commitment from him, so that she would feel able to trust him completely again. She sensed that he was in fact willing to give her that. The way forward was through much more open communication between them.

Looked at from this perspective, Mary could see that there was opportunity for personal growth for both of them. In addition to quality time together, being more demonstrative with her affection and overtly appreciating Geoffrey's best qualities were two important steps that she had to make. Of course, the type of response was up to him, but Mary would be increasing the chances of a warm one.

Renewing the flow of love and goodwill

This was the visualisation that Mary used to complete the process of forgiveness.

Find a quiet place, relax and close your eyes. Allow an image to form that represents for you the concept of loving goodwill. Become aware of the energy that permeates this loving image. What kind of energy is this? How does it flow? Does it have a colour?

Visualise this energy of loving goodwill flowing towards you. It surrounds you with warmth and light. Now it filters through your being until it reaches the parts of you that were so hurt. Experience these wounded parts being caressed by the loving energy until they begin to feel better. Allow plenty of time for this healing process.

If you are able, call to mind the person who harmed you. Perhaps see that this individual, too, has vulnerable aspects. Renew your commitment to yourself to supply whatever the person so cruelly denied you. Recognise what you have learnt through this unhappy episode.

Picture the individual vividly and imagine that the energy of loving goodwill overflows from yourself towards him or her. See the person encircled with this curative force. Now you know that you have been able to forgive.[4]

You may have to repeat the first part of this exercise until your injured thoughts and feelings are comforted. Only then will you be ready to allow the energy of loving good-will to overflow to the person who so distressed you.

The stages of forgiveness

To summarise, the steps you will need to take to complete the forgiveness process are as follows.

> Deal with the strong negative feelings in a safe way.
> Become aware of what it was that you wanted from this person, but did not receive.
> Find a way of meeting this need.
> Be open to considering how you might have contributed to the situation.
> What would be the very best outcome for all concerned? How might this be achieved?
> What have you learnt?

What opportunities are there for personal growth?
Use visualisation to experience the wounded parts
of yourself being healed.
Allow this energy to overflow to the person or
people involved.
You have now forgiven and will experience release.

PSYCHOLOGICAL PROTECTION

Alice reminds me of an elf. She has delicate, pointed
features, cropped brown hair, and a delightful grin when
feeling cheerful. Today, however, she wants to talk about
the invasive energies which she sometimes experiences
emanating from other people. Her usual reaction is to
make herself as small and as invisible as possible, but the
disadvantages are that others find her elusive and making
friends is more difficult. She very much wants to feel
more open and approachable, but how can she do this
without allowing herself to become too vulnerable?

I assured her that this was quite possible using visualisation. Being a very sensitive person, she needed to
learn how to protect herself psychologically, so that even
if people were hostile, sarcastic or otherwise aggressive,
their negative energies would not harm her. Feeling
reassured, she was eager to work with the following
fantasy.

The silk garment
Silk has the reputation of being very protective. In this
exercise you can imagine any type of silk garment, such
as a vest or a shirt, but it must cover the vital organs.

Settle yourself in a place where you feel absolutely secure and where you will not be interrupted. Close your eyes and relax deeply, knowing that you are about to learn how to provide yourself with psychological protection.

Recall any disturbing situation in which you have felt invaded by hostile energies. See yourself there and evoke the other person or people. What did they do or say? How did you feel? What were your reactions?

Now picture yourself walking away from the situation until you find yourself outside an attractive old house. You have heard that it belongs to a wise old person. The door is open and no one is about, so you decide to explore. You climb the stairs to the top floor, which is light and airy. The sun shines through a window illuminating an old trunk. You open it and see that it contains some beautiful clothes. You are particularly intrigued with a silk vest or shirt and take it out. You admire the fine material and are attracted to its colour. You try it on and find that it fits perfectly. You feel elated by this discovery and have a sense that it was meant just for you.

You see a movement in the corner and realise that the owner of the house has been there all along. The person smiles and says, 'I've been expecting you. Take it. It's yours. The silk will protect you from harm. Wear it whenever you feel the need.' You thank the wise person, and continue the conversation in any way that seems appropriate.

You say goodbye and leave the house, still wearing the garment. You return to the difficult situation, but this time knowing that the silk will protect you. As the hostile person or people mock you or look at you with disdain, you see that their words and glances are unable to penetrate the silk, but simply bounce off it. You withstand their aggression with calmness and dignity, knowing that they cannot hurt you. Notice how their antagonism gradually diminishes.

Allow the situation to fade, then find a safe place to keep your precious silk garment. Affirm to yourself that whenever you feel threatened you will put it on, confident of its protective powers.

Alice decided to buy herself a silk vest to reinforce the imagery. Whenever she had to face a difficult situation she would wear it, and found that it gave her extra confidence. No longer did she feel diminished by other people's belligerence.

Another strategy that Alice adopted was to imagine herself inside an invisible bubble, which no hostile forces could penetrate. She also carried with her a crystal which she believed would ward off unwanted energies.

RECHOOSING YOUR PARENTS

Psychotherapy sometimes comes under attack for blaming personal problems on parents. While it is of fundamental importance to take responsibility for ourselves whatever has happened to us in the past, we nevertheless sometimes carry anger and resentments towards our parents for failing to meet our needs as children, or even, in some cases, for abusive, aggressive or unduly critical behaviour which may have resulted in lasting damage.

Sadly, my practice is no different from any other in that many clients have good reason to blame their parents. Often the feelings of anger are mixed with guilt in case they have unwittingly provoked the bad behaviour, so great is the wish to see the adults around them as intrinsically good and caring. Children find ways of coping with difficult situations at home as best they can, at an age when their social skills are very limited. Equally, most adults try to do the best job possible in parenting, given their own history and particular circumstances. Since we learn how to be parents from the ways in which we ourselves were parented, such lessons may serve us and our own children well or ill depending on the messages and experiences passed on.

Sometimes clients tell me that they feel duty bound to visit their parents or in-laws, but dread the occasion, unable to set aside disturbing, intrusive feelings. The following technique has proved helpful in many cases.

The Martian

When visiting the family home, pretend that you are a Martian who has just dropped in from outer space. You are on a journey of discovery and regard everything and everyone with the utmost curiosity. Before arriving at your destination, take time to familiarise yourself with this perspective.

This Martian poses lots of questions. Who exactly are these people? What makes them tick? What influences have formed their characters? What were they like as children? How did their parents treat them? What crises and traumas have they endured? Why do they now behave towards each other in the ways that they do? How have cultural influences played their part? Continue to ask such questions either overtly, or silently to yourself, and note the answers.

As a Martian you are also sensitive to atmosphere and the hidden meanings behind the body language. What messages are these people sending each other, without actually speaking the words? What signals do they give about themselves and how do others respond to them? Because you are a Martian you are not involved and therefore have no need to make any judgements. You simply observe.

You realise that this family tries to tug you into their emotional circle, but rather than be drawn into any conflict or ill feelings, you zoom up to the ceiling in your imagination and survey what is happening. Martians are very clever at adopting this detached perspective!

After your visit, write down everything you have learned about these people and about yourself. How do you now need to live your life?

Eventually, with increased understanding, you may feel able to accept your parents for who they are, and even to thank them for the lessons they have provided, however hard these may have been.

GRIEVING AND LETTING GO

It was late afternoon and three small children were running around in the garden playing tag. Every so often there were whoops of joy as the next person was caught and became 'it'. That morning they had said goodbye to their grandpa for the last time. They had taken an active part in his funeral, read poems for him and laid specially chosen flowers on his coffin. Then they had planted bulbs for him in the garden. Before his death they had been encouraged to visit him in hospital and say whatever they wished. Their parents had facilitated expression of their sad feelings through drawing. These children were therefore able to accept his death as a natural process, allowing them to continue happily with their own lives.

Not everyone is so fortunate. Loved ones may be snatched away unexpectedly through an accident or acute illness. Partners may decide to leave their families, causing feelings of abandonment and grief. If you are faced with the difficult task of having to say goodbye, it is essential to allow yourself to go through the mourning process and complete any 'unfinished business', otherwise the burden of grief or bitterness may be carried with you.

Even if you had no opportunity to say whatever you wished to the person concerned, you can instead evoke the individual in your imagination and complete your dialogue in this way. Then you will be able to let him or her rest in peace. Ritual is a very important part of saying goodbye. Simple acts such as planting bulbs or a tree, or of lighting a candle, can be most comforting.

Molly had always wondered why it was that she was so resistant to completing any academic course work. When she spoke about her earlier life it transpired that her older brother had been killed in a car crash when she was just fifteen. He had been a brilliant medical student and the family had high hopes for him. Believing that they were protecting Molly's feelings, her parents persuaded her not to go to the funeral. Indeed, she found herself in the situation of having to cope with their grief, leaving no opportunity for her to express her own.

Although Molly had done quite well at school, she decided not to go on to college but instead went abroad as an au pair. Subsequently she became a nursery teacher, then married and raised her own two children.

Now she felt restless. She was developing an interest in nutritional therapy and had started a course, but had been unable to finish it. Why was this? After several sessions Molly realised that her brother had been identified as the clever person in the family. She, however, seemed to have been given the role of looking after people's feelings. Her parents had never praised her for school achievements, so she had learnt not to value them. There seemed to be a hidden message that she was not allowed to be as clever as her brother. Despite his death, she was still unconsciously restricting herself. Moreover, it was significant that she had never had the opportunity to grieve for him, which would have freed her to live her own life more fully.

I explained that it was never too late to complete the mourning process, and encouraged her to visit his grave. Meanwhile we performed a Gestalt exercise, imagining that her brother was sitting in the chair opposite her.

'So here is your brother, Patrick. Take a few moments to evoke him, then describe him to me.'

'He's sitting casually, with legs crossed, and is wearing grey cords and a black and white jumper. He has dark hair which flops down over his eyes and every so often he pushes it back.'

'What is his expression?'

'It's difficult to say because he's reading and is preoccupied.'

'Is he aware of your presence?'

'Not really.'

As she said this, I noticed a catch in her voice and asked her what her feelings were.

'Left out. Ignored.' Then, after a pause, she said with some surprise, 'Actually I feel angry with him.'

'What's that about?'

'It seems as if he doesn't think I'm worth talking to. I know I'm seven years younger, but I'm not stupid.'

'Is there something you would like from him?'

'I want him to give me his attention, to talk to me.'

'Tell him.'

'Talk to me! You're my brother and I look up to you.'

'How does he respond?'

'He just turns away and buries himself in his book.'

'How does that leave you feeling?'

'Furious! I want to snatch the damned book away from him.'

'Then do it.' Molly grabbed the imaginary book from Patrick's hands and lashed out with it. After that it was evident that a struggle ensued, with Patrick the victor, but then Molly started to laugh uncontrollably.

'What's your laughter about?'

'At last he's been forced to pay me some attention, that's what. I wish I'd done that long ago, but I was too timid.'

'So now that he's noticing you, say whatever you wish.'

'I want you to know that I'm not stupid and that I can do as well as you in exams, but I need your encouragement. I just need your appreciation and a bit of help.'

'How does he respond now?'

'He says something like, "OK, sis. You could probably do well too if you made the effort. If you want any help you only have to ask".'

'And how does that leave you feeling?'

'Astonished!'

I then suggested that Molly switch roles with her brother by sitting in his chair and taking on his identity. What are the thoughts and feelings from this position? Molly indicated that he had been deeply disturbed by her birth, because until the age of seven he had been the only child. Moreover, she had been a very pretty infant and had gained much attention from relatives and family friends. Subsequently he had learnt to win approval through academic achievement and little sister had been careful not to tread on his toes. In the process he had cut himself off from warm feelings.

Having identified with him in this way, Molly began to understand that life had not been so easy for him and that she had unwittingly initiated the competition between them. She wanted to say sorry and offer him a gift of warm feelings; in return he gave her the power of the intellect.

When she went to visit his grave she took with her a heart of flowers and in her imagination thanked him for allowing her to open to her intellect. She now felt free to go back to college and complete her course. This way Molly was able to make her peace with her brother.

Saying a genuine goodbye can involve deep feelings, so if you decide to follow this exercise then make sure that you look after yourself. Take it at your own pace, just a step at a time if necessary.

Saying goodbye

Evoke the person you wish to mourn, let the individual sit in a chair, and fill in the details of clothes, body posture and facial expression. Check in with your feelings.

Give yourself time to tell the person how you feel and what your thoughts are. Imagine the response. Is there anything you wish you had said before the person died? If so, take this opportunity now.

What do you most want from this person? Can you make a request? What happens? Would you like to offer the person something?

Switch places and take on the identity of the other person. What is that like? How do you appear from this position?

As the other person, what do you want to say to your real self? How do you answer? Do you wish to ask for something or offer a gift?

Go back to your original position and check whether there is anything else you need to say or do to complete any 'unfinished business'.

If you wish, write about this experience.

Create a meaningful ritual based on this imaginary conversation which will help you to conclude the mourning process.

Chapter 5
A Rewarding Working Life

Which subpersonality do you take to work?

Avoiding breakdown.

Coping with authority figures.

Your relationship to time and money.

Surviving interviews and tests.

Developing your creativity.

Yesterday evening I was idly watching a fashion programme on television, which gave advice to ordinary people about how to improve their image. A twenty-one-year-old college graduate was about to begin her first job and wanted to know how to make the transition from casual student and the comfort of trainers, jeans and charity-shop jumpers, to slick office girl with stylish haircut, smart suit and polished shoes. I was fascinated. This was not just about clothes, but about identity. Here was a subpersonality in the making! At first she made loud protests at the high heels and pencil-slim skirt, complaining that she would feel too restricted in such an outfit. In the end she compromised with a smart/casual look in which she was still able to feel comfortable.

It is well worth asking yourself who within you goes to work as this may give you a number of insights about how you feel when there, how you relate to colleagues and how effective you are in that environment.

Many years ago, when I was filling in time as a secretary, I kept wondering why it was that I often felt so annoyed and irritated, especially with anyone holding a position of authority. Having heard about subpersonalities, it took only a few moments to discover that I had taken my rebellious child into the office with me. This rebel hates being told what to do. Being quick-witted she also detests lengthy explanations because of the implication that she is insufficiently intelligent. On such occasions all she wanted to do was stamp her foot and shout, 'I'm not ignorant!' Instead she might find herself wandering off before the explanation was finished. There was also much finger-tapping and banging of drawers, indicative of the restless energy of this subpersonality. Slack moments would be spent secretly reading with the book held under the desk. This rebel never wanted to be stuck in a boring office where there was no scope for originality. Needless to say the job soon came to an end. The lessons were clear: I needed to have autonomy at work and the opportunity to use my mind creatively.

Who goes to work?

Close your eyes and see yourself as you generally are in the morning while getting ready for work, whether you are going out or staying at home to do housework or other jobs. How are you feeling – rushed or relaxed, hopeful or depressed? Be aware of your body language and of your facial expression as you look in the mirror. What sort of clothes do you put on? Do they have any effect on you?

Now picture yourself in your work environment. What are you doing? How are you doing it – with interest and pleasure or with boredom? How do you feel about your work? How much energy do you have? What are you like on the telephone? What tone of voice do you adopt? Now see yourself interact with colleagues and your boss. How do you behave? What happens and what are your feelings? Check in with your deepest need in your workplace – is that fulfilled?

What aspects of yourself do you not bring to work? What happens to them?

Switch roles with someone, or pretend to be a fly on the wall. Have a good look at yourself from this perspective. What sort of person do you see? What are your reactions?

Revert to yourself and become fully conscious of the part of you that goes to work. What name would be most suitable for it?

Make a note of any insights. Would you like to make any changes?

At work we very often have to do what someone else asks. This means that we have to adjust our behaviour to an obedient or helpful mode in order to please the boss. This situation can easily evoke the insecure inner child, who is dependent on a parental figure for approval. This may be fine as long as the boss is appreciative, but if gratitude is unforthcoming then this subpersonality will be in constant pain. Such a person will try harder and harder to please, in the hope that one day their worth will finally be recognised. But you must ask yourself if this is really likely in the present situation. If the answer is 'No', then spend some time just observing the sort of people in authority who do give their employees due credit. They will probably have a fundamental belief in themselves, be good at delegating, be well liked by colleagues and be successful in what they do. No doubt you will come up with other important qualities. Write them down, then go in search of such an employer.

A friend of mine admitted that she always took her 'Goody Two-shoes' to work with her. This subpersonality was a paragon of virtue, very hard-working, with everything achieved on time and to a high standard. Moreover, she was always the one who made the coffee and washed up the mugs. Her desk was immaculately tidy and her in-tray empty before she went home at the end of each day. Her overall feeling was one of smug satisfaction. Indeed, everyone said how marvellous she was. Her main problem, however, was that she had enormous difficulty in relaxing, even during her lunch hour, when she would quickly eat a sandwich then continue working. By the end of the week she was in a state of total exhaustion. Luckily she was aware enough to realise that Goody Two-shoes had to take time off. The first step was to let others make the coffee and do the washing up so that she could put her feet up during the break.

A higher managerial level may involve responsibility for very large sums of money and numbers of people. In business, because time is equivalent to money, much work has to be carried out under pressure, and this can evoke a kind of 'Driver' subpersonality. Matthew was such a case. By the age of fifty he had driven himself to a nervous breakdown. Instead of turning up at work one day, he took the Eurostar to France and spent several weeks wandering around Europe. No one knew where he was, not even his wife. Finally, he felt able to write to her saying that he was safe, but seriously unwell. This crisis forced him to reassess his life and he decided to take early retirement. This kind of breakdown can be avoided if the Driver is recognised and modified at any early stage. While such a subpersonality may be of great benefit in terms of high achievement, if it takes over altogether then the individual is in deep trouble. It is essential to allow time for other aspects of the personality to flourish, in particular the parts that enjoy a good laugh and plenty of fun.

Women who look after children and do domestic work at home can sometimes find themselves living a Martyr's existence, particularly if they have given up interesting work and resent doing repetitive chores. Unfortunately, the rest of the family takes the brunt of the suppressed ill feelings, which may come out, either literally or implicitly, as: 'Look how hard I work for you.' Propelled by the need to be important, she makes herself indispensable, and rarely allows anyone to help. The domestic arena is hers and hers alone, in which she reigns supreme. After all, no one else can do things as well as she can. Sadly such a person is likely to wear a haggard, long-suffering expression and to feel permanently hard-done-by. She needs to learn to ask for and accept help and find more fulfilling ways of being important.

Above all, what you want to aim for is balance. If you discover that one part of you is predominant in your work, ask yourself what the opposite is. Make sure that there is plenty of space for the rest of you when you knock off.

COPING WITH AUTHORITY FIGURES

Willingly taking on a high degree of responsibility is extremely testing and many people have no wish to do this. It is far simpler to opt for a lower level and complain about the boss! Wherever we find ourselves in the hierarchy, however, we will feel empowered as long as we stay in touch with our own inner authority. It is all too easy to give it away by projecting it on to others, leaving us vulnerable to difficult feelings such as fear or resentment.

Derek was a fit young man who had recently joined the local fire service. His training had involved crawling through dark tunnels wearing breathing apparatus, finding his way around smoke-filled rooms, or scaling the heights of ladders, yet none of these situations had frightened him. His first call-out had involved cutting someone out of a smashed car and he coped with this equally well. As long as his mind was focused on a practical task, then he never experienced fear. Yet, back at the station, as soon as an officer walked into the room he could feel himself start to sweat and his mouth would go dry. Moreover, he was overcome with feelings of guilt, yet he had no idea where these came from. He despised himself for being so pathetic and could not understand why he should be so strong in many risky situations, yet so weak in relation to an officer. It had even taken a huge effort to come and see me, as he had imagined that I would judge or criticise him, or even laugh at him. What was going on?

Having assured him that I took what he said very seriously and had no intention of judging or criticising in any way at all, and then thanking him for being so honest, I explained that we all carry a small child inside us who can quickly be activated in particular situations. It became apparent, after talking about his early years, that his father had been a very critical person, expecting a high standard of behaviour from his two sons. Derek had been ear-marked as the naughty one and was often unfairly blamed for something which his brother had done. He lived in a state of perpetual anxiety in case he would be punished or told off. This guilty child still resided within him and became uncomfortably present whenever an officer appeared. He immediately supposed that the officer would find something wrong with his work, despite the fact that he was obviously highly valued by colleagues.

Derek agreed that this explanation made a lot of sense, and now wanted to know the solution. He was willing to work imaginatively to experience reclaiming his own inner authority. I put out a straight-backed chair and a pile of cushions and invited him to become the Guilty Child. He sat on the cushions with his head almost buried in his knees, a cowed expression on his face.

'How old are you now?' I asked.

'About seven,' he said.

'And what are your thoughts and feelings?'

'Worried in case I'll get a thrashing, though I don't really think I've done anything naughty, but I may have done. I'm not sure. If my dad is angry with me, then I must be bad.'

'What happens if you try to stick up for yourself?'

'Oh, I couldn't do that. I'd get told off for arguing or fibbing and get boxed round the ears.'

'So you must feel very small and helpless.'

'Yep.'

'There's nothing you can do to help yourself.'

'That's right.'

'What's your deepest need?'

After some thought: 'To be heard and believed.'

I then explained that he was to imagine that an officer from the brigade was sitting on the chair opposite him. How did he now feel?

'Scared in case he'll find fault with me.'

After exploring the thoughts and feelings of the Guilty Child further I suggested that he swap roles and take on the identity of the officer. At first he found this very challenging, but it became easier when he called to mind an officer he genuinely admired. As this person, his posture changed dramatically. He now sat up straight, could look anyone in the eye, felt strong and sure of himself.

'Tell me who you are now, speaking from the first person.'

'I am an officer of the brigade. I'm a married man and have to earn a good living for my family. So I have to be responsible. I'm in charge of a number of men, but I believe they do a good job and I'm on their side. Unfortunately, not everyone perceives me that way. I'm fair and always listen to another person's point of view, even if I don't agree. I'm often in a difficult situation because of financial cutbacks, and I realise that the men don't always get the support and equipment they need to do the best job.'

'How do you regard the Guilty Child on the cushions?' I enquired.

'There's no need for him to feel guilty. I can see that he hasn't done anything wrong. In any case, I'm always willing to hear his side of the story.'

When Derek reverted to his role of Guilty Child, he could now understand that these feelings were no longer appropriate to his present work situation, and that the officer was not at all like his father.

After returning to his client chair, he said that he had felt very good as the officer and could genuinely connect with that air of quiet assurance, that inner authority. Such a person had no need to criticise, shout and throw his weight about, because he was naturally respected. In future, whenever Derek felt he was being overtaken by guilt and insecurity, he would remind himself that these belonged to the inner child, that he was now an adult and could speak with any officer as an equal.

Give me back my power

If you are having trouble with authority figures, you can contact your inner child and discover what is happening, just as Derek did when he sat on the cushions.

Be aware of your age, posture, and your thoughts and feelings. What memories are awakened? If you had a difficult childhood, then some of these may be painful, so remind yourself that these are not happening now and you can no longer come to any harm. What would make your life better? Which adult caused you to feel so small and insignificant? Ask yourself whether you project this figure on to others in authority.

Now think of someone who holds a position of responsibility, whom you admire and respect. Sit in a chair opposite the cushions and take on this personality. Describe who you are. How do you now hold yourself? What is your energy like? What are your most outstanding qualities? What are your thoughts and feelings? How do you regard the child on the cushions? Can you make any recommendations from this position? Connect with your experience of inner authority.

Close your eyes and allow an image to form for this experience of owning your natural sense of authority. Fill in the details in your imagination.

Make a drawing of your image. Place the drawing on the floor and stand on it. Feel the power and strength rise in you as you do this. Affirm that you are also a person of authority who has no fear of others.

Write about this experience in your workbook. How will you now relate to your boss?

WHAT'S THE TIME?

Most of our lives are dominated by time in one way or another, but people respond to it in different ways. It is useful to find out how you relate to time.

I always wondered why deadlines presented such a problem to me. Even though I knew there was a long enough period in which to finish the job in hand, I would nevertheless suffer terrible feelings of panic, convinced that time would run out. The following visualisation helped me to adopt a more realistic attitude towards time. I hope it is useful to you, too.

Father Time

You are concerned about time and have decided to take a walk in the countryside to try and find a solution to your problem. Fill in the details of the landscape in your imagination. After a while you come to the top of a rounded hill and see that a figure is standing there. As you draw closer you realise that it is Father Time. He holds a large egg-timer and sand is running through from the top to the lower half. You notice the speed at which the sand moves and how much there is left at the top. What does this say about your relationship to time – that there is too much, not enough, that it goes too quickly, too slowly? How do you feel about this?

Father Time is willing to help you and give advice, so ask him anything you wish. What is his reply?

How would you like to see the movement of time? Ask him to adjust the flow of sand for you and see it move in the way that you wish. How do you feel now? What have you learnt about yourself? Would you like to make a new resolution?

Is there anything else you would like to ask Father Time before leaving? If so, then go ahead. See him adjust the flow of time once more. When you have completed the dialogue thank him for his help and say goodbye, knowing that you can return and ask his advice whenever you wish.

Leave the hilltop and open your eyes. Write down your insights in your workbook.

When I first met Father Time in this way, sand was running through the timer at a fast pace and the top half was almost empty. I could feel the panic rise in my throat. When I asked him for help, he pointed out that my natural rhythm was a fairly slow one and it was essential to appreciate that. He suggested that I give myself more time than I actually needed for any job, placing equal importance on plenty of breaks to take the pressure off myself, including whole days free.

He then turned the timer over so that the top half was full and asked me whether my feelings changed. To my surprise I found myself saying that there was now too much time and I experienced being at a loose end! A new problem presented itself as to how I might fill it. As I watched the sand run through, however, I realised that I felt very comfortable as it reached the half-way point. I learnt from this that I needed to use my time well, but should not over-burden myself, so that there was a good balance between work and play.

MONEY WORRIES

Malcolm had been very depressed since his building firm had gone bankrupt. Looking back on his business he realised that a major reason for its failure was a fundamental lack of confidence in himself, which had led him to submit quotations that were too reasonable. He was hoping to be able to set up on his own once more, but meanwhile was working for someone else. How could he avoid making the same mistake again?

First of all we put together some affirmations to help build a better internal image of himself. These were some that he came up with:

I do excellent work and deserve to be well paid.

It's fine to submit quotations that have a generous
profit margin.

I am a worthwhile person and I fully deserve to be
successful.

It's OK to do well and make plenty of money.

Malcolm found some of these statements difficult to
believe at the outset. He had been brought up by deeply
religious parents who disapproved of worldly gain and he
had therefore developed an ambivalent attitude towards
money. He felt that he wasn't 'allowed' to be wealthy.
However, if he were to run a successful business, then
the old messages had to be supplanted with more positive
ones.

Malcolm had one particular quality very much in
his favour: he was genuinely interested in other people.
He could use this to his advantage by striking up a good
rapport with customers, finding out in detail exactly
what they wanted. It is well known amongst sales people
that customers are more likely to make a purchase and
pay well for it if they feel that you take a real interest in
their needs. Malcolm was now able to add another affir-
mation to his list:

I like people and am genuinely interested in supply-
ing their building needs in return for good payment.

With practice, Malcolm was able to give himself psychological permission to do well at his business. This was
reinforced with a visualisation in which he imagined
himself submitting a quotation to a customer that incorporated a healthy profit margin. He then pictured the

quotation being accepted and the work being carried out to his usual high standard. The customer thanked him warmly, appreciating the quality of the building, and paid the bill promptly. He repeated this visualisation a number of times, picturing different customers on each occasion.

Finally, he felt sufficiently confident to start up his business again, wisely employing an excellent accountant to support him. While he never made a fortune, at least he was able to earn a comfortable living doing work that he found satisfying.

Now it's your turn to find out your attitude towards money.

Money messages

Close your eyes and transport yourself back to your childhood. Picture your home and the things in it. Was it a wealthy or a poor place? Where did the money come from? How much was there? What were your parents' attitudes towards it and what did you learn from them about money? Was it a good or a bad thing to have? Should it be saved or spent, shown to the neighbours or hidden?

How much pocket money were you given and what did you do with it? Was it less or more than other children received? How much was spent on your clothes and toys? How did you feel about this?

Now fast-forward to the present and check whether your current situation is similar to or different from that of your childhood. What about your own attitudes towards money now? What did you learn from your parents? Are these messages helpful to you in your present life, or do they limit you in some way? Would you like to make any changes?

See yourself at some future time with the amount of money you would ideally like to have. Where are you, who are you with and what are you doing? What is the atmosphere like? How did you manage to achieve this? What are your feelings?

Open your workbook and write down all you have learnt from this visualisation. The more you can build a vivid image of what it is you want, the more likely you are to be able to realise it. Remember that money is rarely a rewarding goal in itself. It may, however, enable you to develop a personal gift, or offer a worthwhile service to others, or indeed be the result of such work. This theme is continued in greater depth in Chapters 6 and 7.

SURVIVING INTERVIEWS AND TESTS

All of us living in the Western economy have to face exams and interviews at some time or other, and many of us find them unnerving. There are some simple imaginative techniques, however, that will help you to succeed at these. First of all have another look at Chapter 2, which gives advice on how to deal with anxiety. Remember that a few nerves can add sparkle to a testing situation, but too many may interfere. You need to decide in advance how you will bracket off unwanted fear. If you have some sort of an interview or test coming up, then consider the quality you most need to help you with this.

Dorothy, for example, had a job interview the following week and was feeling worried about it. She worked as an arts administrator and positions in this field were scarce. She knew therefore that competition would be intense. Moreover, the advertisement had been unclear as to what the work involved so it was difficult to prepare herself. When I asked her what personal quality she most needed, she said it was the flexibility to be able to answer a wide variety of questions. I then asked her to close her eyes and come up with an image for this quality of flexibility. She immediately saw an elastic band that could be stretched into many shapes and sizes. I suggested that she put one in her pocket before the interview and take it with her. Whenever she wished to call on this quality, she could put her hand in her pocket and reconnect with it.

A supportive symbol

After relaxing and allowing your mind to be open, picture yourself at the impending interview. What is this experience like? Who else is there and how are you feeling? What quality do you most need to help you succeed?

When the quality comes to mind, allow an image to form for it. This may be anything at all: an object, person, animal, or abstract shape or colour. Accept whatever appears without censoring it. Allow plenty of time for the image to form.

When you feel ready, make a drawing of it.

Find an object that represents this image and, if possible, take it with you to the interview. Alternatively, put your drawing into your pocket or handbag. Know that this quality will support you. Connect with it whenever you feel the need.

TAPPING INTO CREATIVITY

In the Introduction I gave some indication of how the mind of a creative genius works. It is particularly notice-able that original scientists and inventors allow a similar process to operate as that of the poet or artist. Features common to all are a relaxed and open state, with the rational mind temporarily suspended. Images can then arise spontaneously from the unconscious, which are subsequently employed in the act of creation. In his autobiography, Max Planck (1858–1947), father of quantum theory, described this as having 'a vivid intu-itive imagination for new ideas not generated by deduction, but by artistically creative imagination'. Having an aesthetic sensibility is another hallmark of this process. Henri Poincaré talked about being guided by 'the feeling of mathematical beauty, of the harmony of numbers and form, of geometric elegance'. However, this type of inspiration does not happen in isolation, but often as the result of much forethought. Louis Pasteur (1822–95) summarised this in his statement: 'Chance only favours invention for minds which are prepared for discoveries by patient study and persevering efforts.'

You might sigh to yourself on reading this and say, 'That is all very well, but I am not a brilliant inventor, nor a mathematical genius, nor am I a world-class physi-cist, so how can any of this apply to me?' The point is that we all have these imaginative and intuitive capabili-ties and the same principles do apply. Moreover, most of us have the capacity to put effort into anything that fasci-nates us. Highly creative people have generally been fortunate enough to find themselves in the right kind of environment, in which their originality was allowed to flourish. We have the opportunity to learn from their experiences. So often something prevents or suppresses this natural flair for creativity and it becomes stunted. If we allow it to blossom, then our lives will be greatly enriched, both in our work and also in our relationships.

If you wish to enhance your creativity in any sphere, whether in running a new business, writing an interesting letter, decorating a house, or forming a friendship, begin by finding a quiet place for reflection and take yourself back to your childhood. Ask yourself the following two questions:

1. What influences contributed to my creativity during my early years?
2. What influences hindered it?

Make a few notes in your workbook, then consider your current situation:

3. How do I include creativity in my life at the present time and in what capacity (at work, at leisure, in the home, in my relationships)?
4. What are the special qualities of my personal creativity?
5. How do I regard creativity and how much priority do I give it?
6. Does anything prevent me from expressing it fully?

Write down your thoughts. Next, go on to the following

visualisation which is in two parts. Have drawing materials to hand.

Meeting your creative block

Close your eyes and recall a time when you felt at your most creative. What was happening? Was anyone else present? How did you feel? What prompted that originality? Connect with that special creative energy. What is that like? Do you experience it somewhere in your body? What sensations go along with it? Allow them to surface.

When you have a vivid impression of your creative energy, let an image form. Watch it emerge and take time to capture its various components. What are its qualities?

Open your eyes and let your hand draw your image on the paper, portraying its colour and shape. Keep it next to you and resume the visualisation.

It is springtime and you are in a hay meadow just as the wild flowers are beginning to open. You have with you your symbol of creative energy. Explore the meadow together and be mindful of your thoughts and feelings.

This meadow is on the edge of a deep forest. What sort of trees grow there? You can see that a path runs down to it. As you both survey the forest you notice something coming into view and you know instinctively that this is the block to your creativity. What form does this block take? What are its particular features, its qualities? How do you react and how does your creative symbol respond?

The block approaches you along the path. What are your feelings? You want to express something to it, so go ahead. In this imaginative world it is possible to have a conversation with any image. Let the dialogue evolve and take the opportunity to make requests of it, if you so wish. Be aware of how your creative symbol responds to the block. Does it want to join in the dialogue? What does it want? Watch the two interact.

Is it at all conceivable that the block might be able to give you anything beneficial? If so, how can this best be incorporated into your creativity without hindering the flow? What does your creative symbol have to say about this?

When your conversation is finished, ask yourself what you have learnt from this encounter. Is there anything you might genuinely thank the block for? Watch it return to the forest and check whether there is anything further that you wish to say to your creative symbol, or it to you. Remember that you can re-evoke your creativity and its block whenever you wish.

Open your eyes and write about this experience in your workbook. Make a sand picture (see Introduction).

When I first performed this exercise, I was in desperate need of help with a major piece of writing. I was up against a tight deadline, yet it was totally impossible to continue. I tried to force the words out of myself, but nothing came. As time went by my panic increased. It was agonising. I spent a whole fortnight just staring at blank pages or at sentences that refused to flow. The harder I tried and the more anxious I became, the more the process of writing eluded me. In the end I gave up and turned to meditation.

My image for my creative energy was a glass full of champagne bubbles and the block was a huge millstone which came rolling out of the forest. How well I recognised it! This symbolised the way in which my natural spontaneity had been suppressed at boarding school, ground down until only conformity remained. Yes, my logical mind had been encouraged and I was grateful for that, but there had been no room for originality. To my surprise, by meeting the block and working with it rather than trying to fight it, I found a way forward. The gift was that it had obliged me to stop and review what I was doing. Rather than attempting to force the words out of myself, I needed to allow my mind to relax so it could once more be free-flowing and spontaneous, like my champagne bubbles. I needed to trust the intuitive part of my mind to do the work for me. I had to let go of all the effort so that this could happen. The next day my writer's block no longer bothered me.

A source of inspiration

Max Ernst (1891–1976), the German surrealist painter, was staying at a seaside inn. He was kicking his heels with frustration as the weather was too wet for excursions. Wondering what to do his eye was drawn to the floorboards, which had an accentuated grain due to the many times they had been scrubbed clean. In a state of excitement he threw down some pieces of paper at random and made a number of rubbings with blacklead. As he concentrated on the resulting patterns and smudges, he found his visionary powers heightened and innumerable images formed themselves before his eyes: human heads, different beasts, a battle ending in a kiss, sea and rain, earth tremors, small tables around the earth, the sphinx in its stable, trickles of lava, scarecrows, and so on. During this process, which he later referred to as *frottage*, he excluded conscious direction of his mind, allowing the shapes in the rubbings to appear spontaneously. From these he created new works of art.

While you may have no aspiration to be a painter, such a procedure can be adapted to help with everyday tasks. For example, when beginning this book I felt overwhelmed with the amount of work to do. What did I need to help me with this venture? My workroom is in the loft of an old barn, and the bricks directly in front of my desk are pitted and scribed with centuries of wear. Whilst reflecting on these, different images revealed themselves: insects, faces, tools, a sailing shop, a small house and various animals. It was the head of an elephant, apparently feeding itself, that captured my attention. When considering its qualities, I realised that it was answering my question. Firstly, I needed to take good care of myself. Also, like the elephant, I required endless patience and steady persistence to complete the book. It would be useless trying to create it in too much of a rush. Whenever I felt frustrated at the slow pace of work, therefore, I visualised the ambling gait of the elephant, realising that this allowed plenty of time for the ideas to flow.

Here is a summary of the method I used.

Asking the images for guidance

Find an irregularly textured surface, such as grained wood, scratched bricks, ink blots, dense foliage, clouds, flagstones, etc. Alternatively, sit in front of a log or coal fire.

Consider what you need help with at this time and ask a specific question. Suspend all logic and reason.

Reflect on the chosen surface, make a rubbing if appropriate, or stare into the fire, and let the images appear of their own accord.

Choose the one that holds the greatest interest for you. How do you feel towards it? What are its chief characteristics? Does it have a message for you? If so, how can you apply this to your problem?

As you will no doubt appreciate, this technique offers yet another way of making available to you the information held in your unconscious.

Chapter 6
Finding Meaning and Purpose

A point to your existence. In touch with joy.

A vision of your future.

Connecting with your potential.

Broadening your horizons.

The hidden meaning of crises. Messages from dreams.

Sometimes people come to see me, often in middle-age, and they say, 'There must be more to life than just this.' They are vaguely dissatisfied, but don't know why. All meaning seems to have gone from their lives. They carry on mechanically, everything seeming point-less. They have lost all sense of purpose.

Further investigation may reveal that boredom has set in after staying too long in the same job, but an over-riding need for security prevents exploration of other avenues. Sometimes there have been previous goals, but these have now been achieved, such as children growing up and leaving home, a top managerial position or a headship in a school. Perhaps there has been a redun-dancy. All that remains is a vacuum.

I know from working with people and from my own experience just how crucial meaning is. As humans, we need to have some sense of purpose. We need to find a point to our existence, otherwise we can easily sink into darkest depression.

However deep your feelings of futility, it is possible to find a way forward. There may be a part of yourself that has never had a chance to express itself. If you look back over your childhood, you will realise that the grown-ups around you encouraged certain natural abilities and gifts that you displayed, but ignored others. Because, as a completely dependent little creature, it was in your interest to please those adults, you developed the capacities that they wished you to have, while other talents remained dormant.

You can witness this if you watch the interactions between parents and young children. Only the other day my three-year-old step-granddaughter sat down at my piano and started to press the keys, expressing great delight at the sounds she was making. Her father was immediately encouraging. Later he admitted to me that he had always wanted to learn the piano, but that as a small boy football had seemed much more important. He would be only too glad if his daughter were to show musical talent. So this little girl is likely to have any such gift warmly supported. But what will happen if she is better at maths or science? And what about her younger brother? In our culture boys are 'supposed' to prefer football to music. Yet it may be that he turns out to be the more musically gifted of the two. What then?

Often, deep feelings of pointlessness set in when we go through life doing what others expect of us, at the expense of our true selves. We may have spent so many years being the sort of person that our parents or teachers wanted, that we have lost track of who we really are. We became so expert at adapting ourselves to other people's wishes that it is only too easy to repeat this as an adult with our partner or spouse. And so that unexpressed potential becomes even more deeply buried.

Yet it is precisely here, with the unfulfilled potential, that meaning may be found. However obscure it may now seem, it is quite possible to reconnect with it and begin to tap into that resource. It is never too late.

As a preliminary exercise, it is worthwhile spending a few minutes reflecting on your upbringing. Make some notes about what was fostered and what was not. What were the expectations of your parents or carers and teachers? To what extent did you conform? Was there anything you longed to do, but never had the opportunity to explore? Perhaps parents were not really interested, were far too busy, or maybe there wasn't enough money. Or maybe you sensed that one or other parent wanted you to fulfil something for them, to achieve something that they may have failed at, or were unable to pursue. Close your eyes and re-evoke the atmosphere at home. What was wanted from you? What was denied?

The following exercise may help you to deepen this inner exploration and to reconnect with that lost potential.

The Time Machine

Imagine yourself standing in front of a door. On the door are written the words 'Time Machine'. Have a close look at the door before opening it. What are your feelings? Now experience yourself walking through the door and entering the room beyond. Have a look around and take in the details of this place. You see a large screen and some knobs and dials. You are curious about what might appear on the screen, so you sit down in front of it and turn the knob that says 'on'. Some images appear, and as you look, you realise that your current life is being portrayed. What are you like? What are you wearing? Who are you with, or are you alone? What are you doing? What feelings do you express? Just watch a while without judgement.

You now notice a dial which you start to turn to the left. The view on the screen is changing and you are aware of turning the clock backwards until you see yourself in the past, about ten years ago. Where are you now? What is the environment like? What do you look like? Are you in any way different from the present? Are you with the same people or not? What is happening? What thoughts and feelings predominate? Were there any difficulties? If so, how did you cope?

Turn the dial again, and, if you haven't already reached it, go back to young adulthood. What were you striving for then? What were your ambitions, your hopes, your fears? How do you appear at this time? How did you define yourself as a man or a woman? What feelings did you have about yourself?

The next swivel of the dial takes you to adolescence. What was life like then? What sort of problems were you struggling with? How did you cope? Was there anyone there to encourage or support you? What were you trying to discover?

Now turn the dial until you reach childhood. See yourself with your family and recall what that was like. What sort of atmosphere was there at home? What is your relationship with the different members? Who is closest? Which person is the most remote? Did you have any pets? What are you doing? What do you look like?

As you keep moving the dial to the left you become

smaller and smaller until you are back in the womb. You see the tiny foetus on the screen, full of potential. Another rotation takes you right back to the very moment of your conception, when the sperm met the egg. As you watch this happening, you realise that a Guardian is appearing, a being who truly cares for you and wants only the very best for you, who will be there to guide and advise you throughout your life. As the being emerges, you realise that it has a special message for you about your life's purpose. Listen to what that is. Ask some questions. Wait and see if there are any other messages or signs that your Guardian wishes to make. When your conversation is complete, say goodbye and watch it disappear from the screen, but know that it will always be at hand to guide and advise you.

Now start to turn the dial to the right, and watch your life gradually unfold from childhood to the present, but this time see everything in the light of the Guardian's messages or signs. Remember that you can consult it whenever you wish. Are there any changes? Do you notice any recurring patterns? What lessons are there for you?

Observe yourself in the present once again and ask yourself: 'What is my life's purpose?' See if an image comes up on the screen in answer to this question. At this stage it may just be a vague colour or shape, but that's fine. Take in the details of the image, then, when you feel ready to close the machine down, turn the knob that says 'off'. Leave the room in your imagination, close the door behind you and open your eyes.

You may like to make notes about what happened, and draw the image that you had at the end of the exercise. Look carefully at the image and list the qualities that it displays, for example whether the colours are bright or pale. Does it give you any clue as to the way forward? What associations do you have with this image? What kind of future do you now expect for yourself, bearing in mind that you have a Guardian to counsel you? Is there any change, however subtle, from your previous expectations of yourself? Are you now aware of any hidden potential that you would like to explore? If so, what is the smallest step that you could take to bring it into being?

LET YOUR HEART SING

When looking back at your childhood, did you recall anything that truly made your heart sing? If not, give yourself a few minutes to reflect on this now and see what comes up from your memory. From an adult perspective it may appear to be something quite childish, but refrain from making judgements because it could be a clue to a happier future. Some people remember the thrill of riding a new bicycle, a trip to the seaside, dabbling in a pond, making model aeroplanes, hearing a beautiful song, and so on. It can be absolutely anything as long as it gave you a glorious feeling of immense pleasure. Children have a natural capacity for play, joy and fun. It is sad indeed that our Western culture fails to value these as important ingredients of adult life. Yet experimentation in the form of play is one of the prime routes to creativity. What we must lose by relegating such spontaneous forms of delight to the under-tens!

When you recall something, ask yourself how you can include that kind of pleasure in your everyday existence.

This may be for recreation, or it may even provide a clue as to a new sense of purpose. Certainly it will contribute to your happiness. Visualise yourself bringing this dimension into your life. Fully appreciate the difference it will make. You may need to repeat the visualisation several times before it becomes a reality.

One client, whenever he feels depressed, goes up to his attic where he has a model railway. An hour or two of play here helps to shift his mood. Another reconnected with her love of flowers, joined a gardening club and made many new friends.

In touch with joy

To summarise the above process, first relax as usual and cast your mind back to your childhood. Recall a time of spontaneous joy. What was this experience like? Where were you? Who else was there (if anyone)? What were the circumstances and what prompted this feeling of elation? Allow yourself to recapture fully the experience of those precious moments.

Now let a symbol come to mind for that joy. What is its colour, its shape, its texture? Does it have a smell or a sound? What other qualities does it have? What are your feelings towards it?

See yourself bringing these qualities into your life. How might you do that? What form do they take? Make a commitment to yourself and be specific about when, where and how you will do this, taking the smallest step in the first instance. Picture yourself as an adult expressing the quality of joy.

Open your eyes and draw your symbol.

LIFE IN FIVE YEARS

We often experience ourselves as being at the mercy of life, rather than being its creator. While certain external factors may be beyond our control, we can nevertheless choose how to respond to these. It is generally true to say that most of us are able to determine our own futures to a far greater extent than we suppose, but we must first of all visualise what we would like the years ahead to hold for us. Without that vision, we have nothing to aim for.

I sometimes ask my clients: 'If you could wave a magic wand, how would you like your life to be in five years, supposing that money and time are no object?' I encourage them to include even far-fetched ideas, because these may spark off others that are more realistic. This process can open you up to new prospects and opportunities and provide a different, more positive perspective on life.

Paul had been working for the same telecommunications firm for the past twenty years, stuck in middle management with no further hope of promotion. He was admonished by those above him if a member of his team was ineffective, and blamed by those below for being insufficiently supportive. He felt like piggy-in-the-middle. It was time to consider a major change of direction. When he waved his magic wand his future looked totally different: he had retrained as an acupuncturist and was leading a rewarding life helping to cure people of chronic health problems. As a result of this visualisation, he enrolled on a part-time course and was planning to take some leave to go to China. When I met him again three years later, he looked a totally different person, with energy and sparkle in his eyes. Although he was as yet unable to give up his full-time job, this was beginning to look possible in another year or so, when he proposed setting up his own practice.

How would you like your life to be in five years' time?

The magic wand

Allow yourself to day-dream. See yourself with a magic wand that sparkles as you hold it. You are going to create a vision of yourself as you will be in five years' time, having already achieved everything that you could possibly desire. Give yourself permission to create a picture of the sort of life that will be totally rewarding. Remember that neither money nor time present any difficulties.

What will your environment be like? See yourself in this place. What are its qualities? How do you feel here? Who are the people you choose to share your life with? If no one specific comes to mind, then which characteristics in others are most important to you and why? How do you relate to these people?

Will you be working? If so, what kind of occupation do you seek for yourself? In what ways will this be fulfilling? Will you carry this out from home or some other environment? What sort of colleagues would you like to have? If you prefer not to be in paid employment, then what is your special contribution to your family, friends or community?

If specifics are difficult to imagine at this stage, such as a different job or relationship, then think of the qualities you would like to have in your life – more friendship or fun,

*perhaps, or maybe creativity or even solitude – whatever
you personally wish for.*

*When you have built a fresh vision for yourself, wave
your wand and see yourself as you will be, with the desired
qualities. Become aware of your feelings. Hold on to this
experience for as long as you wish.*

*Open your eyes and write a description of your life as
you would like it to be in five years. Make a list of the
important qualities. You can, of course, add to your list as
you think of something else, so keep it readily available.
Consider what changes will be necessary. What is the first
step towards your new life?*

As you build this vision of a better future for yourself, it
will gradually permeate your unconscious and you will
become more alert to opportunities as they occur and will
feel positive towards them.

A NEW DIRECTION

Rather than becoming bogged down in the mundane
details of each day, it often helps to stand back and
picture life as an on-going journey which clearly has a
destination. This can be especially helpful if we are
unsure of our next step, or if we feel we have lost our
sense of direction.

You will need five sheets of drawing paper by you,
one for each part of the following exercise, and plenty of
coloured crayons. Allow about an hour for the visualisations, drawings and processing. Cover up the questions
listed below, revealing just one at a time so that you can

focus on it. Ask yourself each question in turn and, with your eyes closed, allow an image to form in answer to it. When you can see the image in all its details, whether it is just a vague colour or shape or something more specific, then draw that image. Ask yourself the next question, allow an image to form by way of reply and draw that . . . and so on until the five stages are complete.

First of all take a few moments to consider your life as a journey. You are part way along the route. Allow yourself to reflect on this. What is this journey like? Do you want to continue along the same route, or do you wish to go in another direction? If so, what would that be like?

Now contemplate each of the following questions:

1. Where have I been on my life's journey?
2. Where am I now?
3. Where would I like to go?
4. What block or obstacle might get in the way?
5. What do I need to help me overcome that block or obstacle?

When the drawings are complete, arrange them in front of you, with the third one last. Study them carefully. How much difference is there between the first and the second? What do those drawings say to you about the kind of life you have been leading? What atmosphere or mood do they express? Have you felt caged in and restricted? Or have you been free to express yourself? What have been the predominant feelings – happy, sad, angry, guilty? How do you currently experience your life? Are there any aspects that leave you feeling discontent or unfulfilled?

Now look at the block or obstacle. This indicates what may prevent you from moving forward. Is it in some way familiar? Is there something in yourself that may hinder you? The fifth drawing may indicate what might help you with this difficulty.

Consider the third picture, your way ahead. In what ways is it different from the first two? What are its qualities? What kind of energy emanates from it? You may have a very clear vision for yourself, or the image may be quite abstract. Nevertheless, the colours and shapes will tell you something.[5]

Occasionally, some people may not be able to visualise their future, and may simply see a question mark, or even nothing at all. If this has happened for you, don't worry. It simply means that the timing of this exercise wasn't right for you. You will have learnt something about the difficulties of your life's journey, and the way forward will become clear in time. Be patient! For the present you will have to accept the not-knowing. Just be aware of what this is like. In a little while you may wish to try The Gate visualisation below.

For others this exercise can be a revelation and a means of finding a fresh path. One client, a jeweller, who was self-employed and found her life solitary, drew for her third picture a house full of people. She longed for the love and warmth of a large family, but her naturally introspective nature prevented her from going out and finding a suitable partner. The quality she most needed was the courage to pursue her own interests in a more extrovert way. The colour that symbolised this for her was a vibrant orange. She then made herself some unusual drop earrings incorporating this shade. She joined a photographic club and wore the earrings to support her at the initial meetings, until she began to make some friends. At her next birthday she invited several of them to a party, already beginning to realise her vision.

Whatever your pictures tell you about your life's journey, write down your thoughts so as not to forget them. Trust whatever it is your unconscious reveals to you. Also keep your drawings in case you wish to add to them or change them in any way.

OPENING TO NEW POSSIBILITIES

Most people find any sort of psychological change alarming, so much so that they prefer to stick with their misery rather than give it up for some unknown way of being. At least their unhappiness is familiar and they know exactly who they are in this state. After all, if their mood were suddenly to change for the better, who would they be then?

If you are having difficulty imagining yourself as different in some way, then just explore what it is like to open yourself to new possibilities. You may find the following visualisation helpful.

The gate
First, check in with your prevailing mood. How did you feel when you got up this morning and considered the day ahead? What were your expectations? Would you like them to be different in any way?

Now evoke a landscape that expresses this mood.
What is it like? Is it hilly or flat, green or barren, warm or
cold? Fill in the details in your mind's eye. Picture yourself
exploring this place.

You have a great yearning to be open to something
fresh, to walk in a different kind of landscape, one that will
help you to feel better, nourished. You notice a path and
decide to follow it. At the end of the path there is a gate.
What kind of gate is it? As you approach you see a sign on
it which reads, 'New Possibilities'. You decide to open the
gate and walk through. As you do this, you realise that the
landscape has changed. You explore this new landscape.
What is it like? In what ways does it differ from the
previous one? What are its main features? How do you feel
in this other environment? What do you most like about it?
What does it give you? Continue to survey it until you feel
familiar with it and comfortable to be there.

It is time to return through the gate. See yourself do
this and be mindful of your feelings. Does the old landscape
seem to have altered in any way?

Write about this experience.

CONNECTING WITH YOUR POTENTIAL

Do you have a sense that a part of yourself became lost at
a time during childhood, that some of your natural abilities have never really been expressed, perhaps because
they were not encouraged or simply because the right
opportunities were not there? It may take some time
before you begin to see your potential with a clear vision,

so do not be disheartened if at first you only have vague inklings. Allow your conscious mind to be receptive and you will tune in to it in good time. A visualisation will also help to speed up this process, such as the one described below.

The waterlily

After settling down in a quiet place and relaxing, allow the image of a pond to come into your imagination. It is very early in the spring and buds are forming on the branches of bushes and trees. A couple of moorhens call to each other as they investigate some possible nesting sites. Take a while to evoke the scene. Now imagine that you are going to have a look at the bottom of the pond. Small creatures scurry about as you descend. There in the mud, not too far from the edge, you see the healthy fat rhizomes of waterlily plants.

You are going to become one of these rhizomes. It is wet and very dark and you have lain dormant here all winter, but now there is a restlessness within you. The water is becoming warmer and you have a great urge to reach for the light, to extend yourself, to grow. First, however, it is necessary to take in the rich nutrients from the mud, so you start to send out some extra roots. At the same time you put up a tender new shoot. You long to fulfil yourself and stretch upwards through the murky water. Then the night falls and you need to take a rest from your efforts.

As the morning light plays on the surface of the pond, the warming rays reach you and you are able to grow towards them once more. You have now put up several strong shoots and each day you energetically reach for the sunlight. As you grow taller, the water becomes clearer and warmer, until at last you reach the surface. Your leaves uncurl and now you can relax and float easily on top of the pond, content to absorb the golden rays of the sun.

The next day, however, you realise that there is more to be done, more of yourself to be fulfilled. At your very centre a bud begins to form. As the nutrients reach you from the dark mud below, the bud grows fatter, until finally the pure white petals burst open. The waterlily has finally flowered.

Imagine now that you separate from the plant and look down into the very heart of this flower that is you. You feel a tender affection for it and, as you look, you are connected to the very highest and best in yourself. You begin to be aware of everything that you may yet become, and as this happens, an image for your potential forms at the centre of the flower. Allow the image to take shape, whatever it may be, and see it fully in all its details. Be attentive to its special qualities.

Ask: 'How can I bring these into the world?' Do you sense a response?

When you feel complete with this visualisation, remind yourself that you can return to this pond whenever you wish and reconnect with your potential. Draw the image and write about what happened.

Consider how you might realise your potential in terms of your everyday life.

BROADENING YOUR HORIZONS

Brenda, by her own admission, had led a sheltered life. She was slight in build and had a soft, somewhat hesitant manner of speaking, but her eyes shone with intelligence. She had done well at boarding school, then during her student years became engaged and married shortly after leaving university. Although her marriage was a happy one, she referred to it as an escape into safety, having found the world in general hostile and confusing.

Having recently passed thirty, however, she was beginning to feel constrained and wanted to know how she could broaden her horizons. Working with imagery was a useful way of setting this process in motion. The following visualisation had a considerable impact on her.

The magic carpet

After relaxing, consider a time when you felt particularly hemmed in or confined. Let yourself recall the situation, where you were, who was there (if anyone), and what contributed to that feeling. You wish to be liberated from this confined place and to broaden your horizons.

As you ask for your wish to be granted, you look up and see a magic carpet flying towards you. You feel excited and want to take a ride on it. It lands near you and you examine it closely before stepping on to it. What is it like? Does it have a pattern woven into it? What colours have been used? Are there cushions on it? Do you sit or stand?

Soon it takes off and you can feel yourself rising upwards. You look back at the place you have just left. What are your feelings? What does it look like from this perspective? What do you like or dislike about it?

Now you turn towards the direction of your flight. You can see the horizon in the distance and have a sense of anticipation. As you watch, the details become gradually clearer. What does it consist of? How does it differ from the place you left? Do your feelings change at all?

As you draw closer, decide whether you wish to land and explore. If so, ask the magic carpet to descend. Where do you find yourself? What are the main features of this new location? What is it like to be here? Do you meet anyone? If so, does the person (or animal) have a message for you?

Eventually you have to return and you remount the magic carpet, taking with you in your imagination the experience of being in this broader place. You know you can make a return journey whenever you wish.

Create a collage of your broader horizons, or a sand picture (see Introduction).

When evoking the feeling of confinement, Brenda had found herself inside a cage. She could see the magic carpet through the bars, but felt panic-stricken in case there was no way out. However, on closer inspection she realised that the padlock to the door was on the inside and the key was hanging on a nearby hook. This symbolised to her the way in which she had created her own prison. Unlocking her cage and stepping out on to the magic carpet was a truly liberating experience for her. The broader horizon contained friendly people from many nations.

After this experience she realised that she wanted to use the languages she had studied and to do some work involving people. She eventually found a rewarding position with a major charity.

CRISES: THEIR HIDDEN MEANINGS

Crises, although difficult and painful at the time, may ultimately reveal fresh opportunities for your own growth. In retrospect they can seem deeply meaningful, resulting in a turning point of some kind that indicates a new way forward. The reason for this is that any major crisis is likely to upset the old patterns and habitual ways of being. As these fall apart and disintegrate, the space is left for something fresh to arise.

A couple of years ago a friend of ours called Jim had a somewhat bizarre accident. He took his girlfriend to a nightclub and, after a few drinks, they began to dance. Becoming somewhat carried away during a fast number, Jim tripped and fell, pulling the young woman on top of him. Everyone thought this was a huge joke, but unfortunately Jim's foot had become trapped and so badly twisted that his ankle broke under the weight of their two bodies. As a result he was off work for three months.

This enforced inactivity provided plenty of opportunity for self-reflection. At last he appreciated how important a well-functioning body was and he decided to become super-fit as soon as he was mobile again. Not only did he give up excess alcohol and smoking, but he switched to a healthier diet and took up long-distance cycling. He became so expert that he was soon beating eighteen-year-olds in races.

Jim now declares that breaking his ankle was one of

the best things that has ever happened to him.

The three crises

This exercise will give you the opportunity to look at how you deal with major difficulties and what sense you can make of them. It might be helpful to remind yourself of the concept of subpersonalities outlined in Chapter 1. Before relaxing, put your drawing equipment by you. If you are able to carry out this exercise with a trusted friend, then so much the better as you can give each other feedback.

Call to mind three crises that you have encountered during the course of your life: one that occurred recently, one from early adulthood or adolescence, and one from childhood. Give yourself plenty of time to consider each in turn. Be attentive to the scenes that appear spontaneously in your mind's eye. When you have recalled their various components, make a drawing of each of the three situations, expressing in particular the feelings, any sense of disintegration or loss, indeed the very essence of what happened to you.

When your drawings are finished, lay them out before you in time sequence, then ask yourself the following questions, making notes about your answers.

A.　1)　*How did I deal with these crises? What were my responses, my style of coping?*

　　2)　*Did I try to postpone or ignore them?*

　　3)　*Did I attempt to hang on in any way?*

　　4)　*Did I face them courageously?*

　　5)　*Did I deal with each differently, or the same?*

B. *Do I recognise any subpersonalities in operation, either suffering from the pain, or taking steps to sort the situation out?*

C. *1) Do I notice a pattern or patterns?*

   2) Is there any sense of continuity, any feeling of development between each crisis?

D. *1) Did any new opportunity arise as a result of each crisis or difficulty?*

   2) What did I do about it: ignore it, postpone it, follow it up?

E. *If there is any learning or communication implicit in these crises, what might it be?*

MESSAGES FROM DREAMS

I awoke with a start one morning, recalling yet another dream about train journeys. This time it was necessary to make a quick change on the way and I was standing on a platform in the north of England in a state of high anxiety. My trunk had to be taken off the first train and put on to another. This second train was about to arrive, yet there was no sign of my luggage. Perhaps the guard had forgotten to unload it, which meant that it was now on its way to the West Country. Was it correctly labelled? I couldn't remember. Moreover, there was confusion about the platform number. In a panic, I rushed to the information office, then to the departure board to double-check on times, realising that this was the last train to my destination.

As it drew into the platform I was in a terrible state of indecision. Should I take the train as planned and leave my trunk behind, hoping that it would eventually reach me? Or should I miss it and find the luggage, bearing in mind that I was in a strange place and had nowhere to stay the night. The sweat was pouring off me when I awoke.

Other train dreams have involved a large black bag containing my most personal possessions. This bag would be lost or stolen, maybe retrieved at the last minute, but the anxiety was always intense. My unconscious seemed to be trying to tell me something, but what could that be? It was only some years later that I was able to decode the message, as a result of my psychotherapy training, which taught me how to work with dreams from the inside. Thus, I stepped into the imaginary world of the train journey and identified with the most significant object, in this case the trunk. This is what I wrote in my journal.

'I am a trunk. I contain everything that Rachel most values and I am therefore extremely important to her. However, she finds me a great worry and responsibility. I am too big for her to carry and she has to rely on others for my transportation. She finds this very scary in case I am mislaid. That would be like losing her most essential self. No wonder she feels so panic-stricken.

'As she changes trains, she is considering a new direction in her life. She wants to take me with her, but others impede her progress.

'If she would open my lid and take out some of the precious luggage for her own use, then I would be much lighter to carry around. Moreover, there would be less need to depend on the guard's cooperation. Perhaps she ought to go back and have another look at the departure board and discover a new, much more rewarding route.'

This was a revelation to me! At the time of the dream I was indeed considering a new direction in my life, but was too frightened to make a major change. Instead of going freelance and leaving the city for the country, which is what I most wanted to do, I simply took another full-time, even more stressful job. Rather than explore the potential that lay locked in the trunk, I continued along a similar route. It was only after I finally left London and became a professional counsellor and writer that the dreams ceased. By then the trunk had been opened and the contents reclaimed.

No doubt you have had many dreams that have left you feeling puzzled as to their meaning. If you wish to understand their symbolism, then step into them just as I did.

Inside a dream

Always remember to write down the details of any dream as soon as you wake up, otherwise you will not be able to retain them. Keep your workbook next to your bed. If you have had a disturbing nightmare, then do not attempt to deal with it on your own. Find a well-trained therapist to assist you.

Proceed as normal when preparing to visualise and make sure you are relaxed and comfortable. Read through your dream before closing your eyes.

As you re-evoke it, imagine yourself there once again. Be aware of your feelings. If you need any help at all, then ask for it and see what materialises.

Look around you and consider which element most

captures your attention. You may like to have a
conversation with it, whether it be a person, animal or
object, to find out more about it.

If appropriate, step into the chosen image and
experience it from the inside. Who or what are you? What
can you reveal about yourself? How do the events of the
dream appear from this perspective? Do you wish to
converse with the dreamer, or any other image? Open up the
dialogue and say whatever you wish. What are your
feelings? Do you sense any deep need here? What is the
response? Can you offer any advice?

Step back into your dreaming self. Have you had any
insights? Would you like to repeat this process with any
other element? Move through the story of the dream and
consider whether you would like to explore other parts of it.
Go ahead. What messages do you receive?

Write down what happened as soon as you open your
eyes.

Some dreams are prompted by ordinary events and hold
little meaning. Others come from deep within the unconscious and are profoundly revealing. What can you
discover through this medium about your potential and
your life's purpose? Ask your intuitive mind for guidance.

Chapter 7
Sailing with the Wind

A symbol for your will. Exerting your strong will.
Being skilful with your will. Extending good will.
The will and spirituality. Meeting the saboteurs.
How to achieve your aims.

The workshop leader was enthusiastic. The topic under discussion was that of the will, the energy behind the action, something that is flowing and dynamic. It is not about forcing or coercion in the Victorian sense, nor is it about repression or power. Rather, it is concerned with the alignment of will energy with one's true purpose in life. When this happens, there is a sense of ease about exerting the will, because everything falls naturally into place. It is like navigating with the wind in your sails, blowing you along in the right direction. This is the psychosynthesis concept of the will. The idea attracted me and I wanted to know more of the theory, but first each individual had the opportunity to discover, through a visualisation, what their personal will was like and how it operated. I found my imagery astonishing.

'I am standing in the middle of a field with a horse. He is magnificent and powerful, with strong muscles evident beneath the gleaming black coat. His name is Jet.

He is restless and wants to go for a gallop, but his field is too small. I promise to take him for a ride and attempt to put his saddle on, but he bucks and throws it off. I then try to push the bit between his teeth, but he refuses to open his mouth and tosses his head proudly. Clearly, Jet has no wish to be restrained in any way, so there is nothing for it but to ride him bareback and cling on to his long, shaggy mane.

'Once on his back I feel exhilarated, and we set off at a fast pace. There is a gate in the corner of the field and beyond it a bridleway. Expecting him to stop while I dismount and open the gate, Jet takes me by surprise by making a huge leap into the air, clearing the top effortlessly. We canter down the bridleway until we reach the sea. The tide is out, leaving a vast expanse of firm sand. Here Jet gallops flat out while I enjoy the thrill of being in tune with his powerful energy.

'Eventually the light begins to fade and it is time to go home. We are tired but happy. Jet retraces his steps to the bridleway and back up to the gate. This time he pauses while I open it and he follows me into the field.'

So how did I interpret this imagery? What could it tell me about my will? I knew instantly that restraint had been a serious problem for me, due to my environment and circumstances. There never seemed to be sufficient room to express what I felt passionately about – or no one else seemed interested. In many respects I had been ahead of my time, for example in becoming a vegetarian long before it was acknowledged by the medical profession as healthy. The imagery also reminded me how headstrong and stubborn I could be once I was set on my own course. While this meant that I usually completed

things, it also indicated a lack of flexibility and willingness to listen to other people's points of view. What
surprised me most of all was the tremendous energy
behind my will! This was something I could utilise to
great advantage.

If you wish to discover more about how you relate
to your will, then make yourself comfortable in a quiet
place and create your own visualisation. What sort of
horse do you see – a quiet pony, a sleek hunter or perhaps
even a carthorse?

The horse

*After relaxing and closing your eyes, focus for a while on
your will. Think of a time when you made an important
decision and carried out the necessary steps. What was that
like? When you feel connected with your will, allow an
image to form of a horse. Picture its size, colour, where it is
and what it is doing. Be aware of its temperament. How do
you relate to this horse? What are your feelings towards it?
Does it have a name?*

*You are going on a journey with your horse, so
consider how to do this. A saddle and bridle are there.
What happens? Allow your imagination to take you on this
journey. Where do you go? What is the landscape like?
How does your horse behave? What are your reactions? Are
you able to guide it with the reins or other commands?
Explore the area together and communicate with each
other. Is there anything you want from your horse? What
are your feelings at this point?*

*Eventually it is time to return, so watch this
happening. How does the landscape now appear?*

Complete your journey, and see if your horse has any

*message for you. Say goodbye and know that you can meet
again at any time if you so wish.*

Write up this visualisation in your workbook. What have
you learnt about your will? Is there any aspect you
would like to develop? What is its main form of expression? Perhaps it falls into one of the categories outlined
below.

EXERTING THE STRONG WILL

When considering the will, this is the first type that
springs to mind. However, in its best form it is not
concerned with aggression or domination, but rather
with assertion and perseverance. It may involve courage
and determination and is generally experienced as ener-
gising and powerful. A strong will is extremely useful if,
for example, we have to carry out a resolution or persist
with something difficult.

　　Do you have access to a strong will? The following
exercise will help you to discover what yours is like. You
will need a clear space as it involves movement. If necessary, have another look at the section concerning
subpersonalities in Chapter 1.

*Stand quietly and recall a time when you exerted a lot of
strong will. What prompted you to behave in this way?
What was your motivation? Did you have some kind of goal
or aim? Did you feel passionately about something? Where
were you and what was happening? Who were you with?
What did you do or say? What difficulties did you*

encounter? What was the outcome? Relive this experience in
your imagination as vividly as possible.

Now check in with what happens in your body and
begin to create a moving image that demonstrates your
strong will. Allow your body to shape itself into this image.
What does that feel like? Move around and make
corresponding sounds. How long can you maintain this?
How easy or difficult is it to exercise your strong will? How
much energy do you have? How quickly do you tire?

Is there by any chance a subpersonality in operation,
an authoritarian or controlling figure, perhaps, that gets
you to do things? If so, then be aware of how helpful or
limiting this part of yourself is.

Without changing your posture, close your eyes for a
while and sense a warm breeze blowing your way. This
represents the strong will in its purest form, simply
regulating and directing rather than controlling or
pressurising. Allow it to envelop you and be aware of
whether your body wants to adjust itself. What happens?
How do you feel now? How much energy do you have?

When you describe this experience in your workbook, include ideas as to how you might exert your
strong will differently in future.

BEING SKILFUL WITH THE WILL

Here again, ease is the catchword. This form of will
concerns the development of strategies that are the most
effective and often involve the least amount of effort. It
may well include expert organisation and diplomacy and
is likely to be enabling and facilitative in nature. Good

timing is important. It does not involve manipulation, collusion or cunning of any kind. If these characteristics are evident, then they are likely to belong to a subpersonality.

I always think of my husband as being skilful with his will in the most ingenious ways. One day he was driving into a nearby town with a colleague when the car broke down in an awkward place. Somehow they had to get it out of the way of the traffic and on to the pavement, but although one pushed hard while the other steered, it was impossible to force it up over the high kerb. John then had the brainwave of putting the car into reverse gear and turning the engine over with the starter motor. This mobilised the wheels sufficiently to make the job easy.

The next visualisation will give you some clues about the skills you deploy when devising ways of achieving something, or alternatively what can go wrong and what you can learn from that. You will need drawing paper and coloured crayons or pens.

Find a quiet place and turn your attention inwards. Call to mind a time when you wanted to achieve something rather difficult, which needed much skill to negotiate and bring into being. What was the situation and what exactly was your aim? Who or what caused the difficulties? Was there anything that you feared? What qualities did you have to find in yourself to ensure success? Picture the situation and the people involved. What happened and what was the eventual outcome? Did you achieve your aim or did something go wrong?

When you feel connected with your skilful will, allow

*a symbol to form in your imagination. Take time to picture
its features and then make a drawing.*

*Reflect on your image. What are its salient
characteristics? What have you learnt about your
skilfulness in exercising your will? Are there any qualities
that you need to develop so that you can be more effective?
If so, then make a conscious decision to bring them into your
life. Write the words on cards and place them around your
room. Read biographies of people you admire who
demonstrate these qualities. Use them as your models.*

EXTENDING GOOD WILL

If you have an urge to make life better for others and choose
objectives that are in line with the common wellbeing of
humanity, then you are in touch with the spirit of good
will. Beware, however, of the Do-Gooder and Martyr
subpersonalities, as well as the Superserver, who rushes
around helping everyone, whether or not such assistance is
wanted. If you suspect that one of these is in evidence, then
evoke it (*see* Chapter 1) and conduct a dialogue with the aim
of discovering what deep need drives that part of you. Is it
for love or approval or something similar? While we can
use aspects of subpersonalities to our advantage, if they
take over then we lose contact with our true will because it
is dominated by their needs. Always check that you have
free choice in the matter, rather than being impelled by
some unconscious force.

Good will in its purest form is unconditional and
non-attached. It is cooperative and caring in a selfless
way.

Think of someone who exercises good will in its best form.
Find a picture of that person and display it in your room to
inspire you.

Create an imaginary conversation with the person.
Ask whatever you wish about exercising good will. What
can you learn from this? How much can you bring this
capacity into your life? How might your life change as a
result?

Consider a small way in which you could exercise your
good will and make a commitment to carry it out.

While good will is in essence about doing something for
others, selfless acts are far easier if you yourself are well
nourished. Martyrs and Superservers in particular need
to learn to look after themselves in the first instance and
to ask for help when necessary, otherwise they are likely
to end up burnt out or ill and then they are no good to
anyone. For this reason I offer such clients the concept of
healthy selfishness. In my own work with people, I am
aware of being much more effective when feeling relaxed
and content inside. As long as I am stressed out or
knotted up with personal problems, then I am not truly
available for others.

THE WILL IN THE TRANSPERSONAL REALM

Is it really possible to link the will with spirituality? On
the surface they appear to be somewhat contradictory,
the one being associated very much with reality and the
other with the insubstantial. However, anyone who has

connected with their true purpose in life needs access to the will in order to bring their spiritual quest or task into everyday life. If you have worked through the previous chapter and now have a real sense of the reason for your existence, then your will is no doubt coming into focus.

To view this connection the other way round, it is often after hard labour and an effort of will that inspiration and illumination can suddenly strike. In more prosaic terms, when the groundwork to a problem has been well prepared and the various aspects mulled over, then the intuitive part of the mind is able to produce the answer one is seeking. This invariably happens out of the blue, as described in the Introduction, such as after a good night's sleep or a stroll, especially when one is feeling relaxed.

Mathematicians in particular have reported the latter phenomenon. A famous example was given by the Frenchman André Marie Ampère (1775–1836), whose name was later to be given to the unit of electric current. In his diary of 1802 he described his first great discovery, which he had worked on for seven years. 'I gave a shout of joy ... I had sought twenty times unsuccessfully for this solution. For some days I had carried the idea around with me continually. At last, *I do not know how*, I found it, together with a large number of curious and new considerations concerning the theory of probability.'

The experience is so striking that it is often referred to in spiritual terms. Karl Friedrich Gauss (1777–1855), a German mathematician, finally proved a theorem after four years of labour, saying in a letter to a friend, 'At last two days ago I succeeded, not by dint of painful effort but so to speak by the grace of God. As a sudden flash of light, the enigma was solved . . . For my part I am unable to name the nature of the thread which connected what I previously knew with that which made my success possible.'

Either way, it is important to align your will with the very highest and best in yourself.

Go back to the Waterlily visualisation in Chapter 6 and remind yourself of the image of your potential. What qualities were you in touch with then? Write these qualities on a piece of paper.

Contemplate the type of will energy you need – strong, skilful or good – in order to realise your potential and bring it into everyday life. Write this down on a separate piece of paper. What kind of energy is this – powerful, gentle, vibrant? Whatever it is, allow the sensation to rise in your body. What does this feel like?

Take hold of the pieces of paper, one in each hand (the will energy on the right if right-handed, vice-versa if left-handed), then close your eyes.

Focus on the qualities first of all. These belong to your potential and are precious to you. You are going to put them in a special bowl. Picture the bowl, evoking all its features, then see yourself carefully dropping the qualities into it.

Now focus on the will energy that your potential needs and be aware of it coursing through your body. Create an image of this will energy in your mind's eye. What is that like – static or flowing, light or heavy? What colours is it composed of?

When you have a vivid impression of this energy, watch it moving towards your bowl and surrounding it. See what happens as it interacts with the bowl and its contents.

Stay with this experience for as long as you wish.
Write about what happened.

THE INNER SABOTEURS

Perhaps you have connected with your purpose and know how you should proceed, but find yourself reacting against it. Maybe too much responsibility is involved, or perhaps you are afraid of becoming too visible in the world. It is useful to discover what obstacles might lie in your path.

When I was recovering from cancer, I knew that it was vital to find a new way forward, another direction in life, if I was to stay well. High-stress managerial work clearly no longer suited me and I knew instinctively that I had grown out of balance with myself. How could I redress that balance and find a healthier lifestyle? The damage to my breast was a powerful symbol for me concerning the loss of my womanhood. How could I reconnect with that and find a new way of expressing my femininity? This needed not only a sense of purpose, but the will with which to carry this out and make the necessary changes. Firstly, it was crucial to find out what might pull me from the path, what the saboteurs might be, so I decided to work with visualisation. This is what I wrote in my journal.

'As I meditate on my womanhood, I see a hill in the distance, and on it there is a sparkling fountain throwing into the air great arches of water which fall in cascades around it. In the fine spray above it a rainbow appears. I am aware of the fluidity and vitality of the fountain, contrasting with the mysterious and somewhat enigmatic rainbow.

'Leading towards the fountain is a straight path, representing my will. I can see myself on that path, but there is a long way to go and I know that I am likely to encounter many obstacles.

'As I walk along the path a raging black monster suddenly appears on my left. It has long fangs and wild black hair. It rises up on its hind legs, snarls menacingly, then attempts to tear at my flesh with its sharp claws. I identify it instantly as my cancer. If it could, it would drag me from the path and carry me to my grave. The vision of my fountain, however, gives me the courage and energy with which to break free and continue on my way.

'On the right there appear two women in white coats. I recognise them as doctors. They tell me to take off my clothes because they have to examine me. Then they explain that to improve my chances of survival they have to suppress the effects of the oestrogen by irradiating my ovaries. The tears roll down my face. I am still in search of my womanhood. How can they take it away before I have even found it? How could they do such a terrible thing to me? I know that this extra treatment isn't right for me, but what if I refuse it? Will I die? Again I connect with the vibrant fountain and the mysterious rainbow hovering above it. They give me the strength to say "No" and I dress myself and walk on.

'Further along the way, I see a man bowed down under the weight of the cross he is carrying. I know this is Christ. He looks miserable. He invites me to join his suffering and tells me that the only road to salvation is through the vale of tears. I tell him quite firmly that I have suffered enough pain and misery and that I am not yet ready to die. A shaft of sunlight falls on my fountain and I announce. "I am on my way to being a beautiful, radiant woman!" I sense that he understands and accepts my words. I experience immense relief and carry on along the path.

'Next I encounter a priest. He stands aloft in his pulpit and is preaching a sermon on chastity. He looks over the top of his spectacles and says, "Be modest and cover up your body. You're sinful, like Eve the temptress. The evil in the world is all the fault of women, who lead men astray. Virginity is a virtue." I struggle with the weight of guilt and disgust with my body, thrust upon me by outmoded religious indoctrination. Then I realise that my fountain is much closer and I am able to speak my mind: "Your sermon does great harm. God made my body and offered me the gift of sexuality, and I'm learning to celebrate it. My womanhood will flower despite you." My step is much lighter as I walk on.

'Then I have to face my mother. "Look what happens to girls who lead men on", she says. "They get pregnant and ruin their lives. Don't ever get pregnant."

'"I've listened to your instructions for far too long, Mother, and have denied my womanhood. I know that you mean well and are concerned about my safety, but I'm no longer a teenager. I am a fully grown adult and can look after myself and make my own choices now. My next step in life is about expressing my femininity in the world. Goodbye, Mother."

'A wave of happiness surges through me and I now run up the hill towards the fountain. I am filled with joy and excitement. This time I long to take off my clothes and stand under the sprays of water, with arms outstretched, to experience the fount of energy flowing through me. Round about, the colours of the rainbow dance and sway. I celebrate my body, my womanhood, and see its energy radiate out towards the world. I stay with this experience for a long, long time until it fills every aspect of my being.'

What pulls me from my path?

Here is your opportunity to discover what might sabotage your aims. Before beginning the visualisation, bring to mind an important goal that you wish to set yourself, then relax deeply in a quiet place and shut your eyes.

Create an image for your goal. See it at the far end of a path along which you are travelling. You know that various difficulties and obstacles are going to block your way or sidetrack you, but despite these you are determined to carry on until you succeed in reaching your destination.

Let the visualisation unfold and deal with each impediment as it occurs. Imagine the images and conversations as appropriate. Note the thoughts and feelings that arise with each encounter. Keep going.

At last you arrive at your goal. How do you feel now? See what happens. What have you learnt from this exercise?[6]

It was through my decision to train as a psychosynthesis therapist that I was finally able to express my womanhood in this caring capacity. Before being able to take such an important step, however, it was necessary to prepare myself both emotionally and psychologically. It was in these areas that I found visualisation so illuminating and helpful.

In working through this chapter, you have had the opportunity to discover much about the nature of your will, what shortcomings there are, what still needs to be developed, and how you can best employ it.

It is now time to bring your dreams for yourself into reality, but first you need to ask yourself whether you are willing to make a conscious new decision.

Am I willing?
Put your drawing tools by your side and settle yourself as usual.

Think of a time when you felt totally willing to do something. Recreate the situation in your imagination, seeing yourself there along with any other people present. What was it you wanted to do? Get in touch with the feelings associated with that willingness. What happens in your body?

Let a symbol appear for your willingness. What is its form, its shape, its colours? Is it something specific or abstract? How does it move? Does it make a sound?

When you can see your image clearly enough, open your eyes and make a drawing of it.

Close your eyes again and search in your memory for a moment when you felt absolutely unwilling to do something. What symbol now appears in your mind's eye? Once again, fill in the details until you become familiar with its various characteristics. When you feel ready, make a drawing of this one too, on a separate piece of paper.

Put the two drawings side by side. What enhances

your feeling of willingness? What benefits and advantages has this brought you? On the other hand, what contributes to your unwillingness? Did you lose any important opportunities or cause yourself or others pain as a result of being unwilling? Which do you currently most identify with?

Continue with the ensuing six stages towards the realisation of your goal only when you feel completely in touch with your willingness.

HOW TO ACHIEVE YOUR AIMS

To give you a clear idea of the sequence of steps involved in making your dreams and visions a reality, I will describe to you what happened for me when first I started to work with the act of will. At the end of each section are notes to guide you.

1. Setting the goal

It seemed sensible to begin with something achievable so that I would feel encouraged by a small success. What I wanted was to feel more in touch with other people, so my aim was to bring the quality of connectedness into my life. In meditating on this quality, the image that came to me was of two hearts joined by a string. As my awareness shifted to my body, 'tautness' was the best word to describe what was happening there, not indicating any nervousness, but rather acute sensitivity, like a perfectly tuned violin.

It was important to ensure that I genuinely wanted to work with this, and to ask myself whether there was a lower as well as a higher motive. There certainly was! My motivation was not entirely altruistic, as I also hoped for love and appreciation from others in bringing connectedness into my life. Did I accept both motivations and did I still want to continue? My answer was in the affirmative, so I could move on to the next stage.

In setting your goal, use visualisation to discover the qualities that are meaningful to you and how you can bring these into your life. Are they in line with your overall sense of purpose? If they are and if you attach great value to them, you will feel inspired to pursue your aim. Alternatively, if a goal has come to you in a flash, then check that it holds qualities that are worthwhile.

Look at both higher and lower motivations and consider whether they are acceptable to you. Do you wish to continue?

2. Deliberating

This involved taking a large sheet of paper, writing my aim in the middle and depicting my image, then drawing a circle around these. This became the body of a large 'spider' with many legs, each of which represented an association to the main theme. Hairs on the legs pointed to peripheral ideas. Allowing my mind to free-associate around the quality of connectedness produced many related images, thoughts and memories, both positive and negative, such as the delightful intimacy I shared with my husband, gratitude to kind neighbours, empathy from members of my cancer support group, closeness to the elemental forces of nature, the pain of involvement with world affairs or feelings of suffocation or embarrassment if other people's demands were too pressing.

It was important to consider the consequences of this act and also to be alert to the subpersonalities that were triggered (*see* Chapter 1) and whether they would be helpful or obstructive. It quickly became obvious that my frightened child, Scared Sonia, was terrified of being sucked into someone else's sphere of influence, of being overpowered or victimised. She would need protection. Equally, my Mr Regulator, who had a liking for schedules, would probably feel threatened by a possible loss of control, and would need reassurance. I learnt from this that being connected and in tune also meant choosing to detach myself and withdraw when appropriate. At the same time, somewhere among those spider legs were the possibilities that pointed towards a more fulfilling future.

Use free association to consider all the possibilities and connections linked to your aim, both positive and negative. Include the desirability and consequences of accomplishing it when working with your 'spider'.

3. Making a choice

This was difficult. I had to select one association on which to focus in the first instance. This meant letting go of alternatives. In the end I chose connectedness to my creativity. Immediately this let loose a flood of criticisms from Priscilla Prim, my fault-finding subpersonality: 'How selfish you are. You ought to be thinking about other people and putting them first. All this navel-gazing isn't doing you or anyone else any good!' and so on. However, I was able to point out to her that through my creativity, by expressing myself through music and writing, my connectedness to others would be greatly increased.

From all the possible goals or ways forward, you have to make a choice and then a decision. This needs to be from a clear and centred place, so be aware of any interference from subpersonalities. Make sure that this choice will not harm yourself or others in any way and that it is in line with your overall purpose in life.

4. Affirming the decision

Before carrying out an act of will, it is essential to have faith in oneself. Doubts and resistances can quickly inhibit the best of intentions. Was my creativity really worth anything? It was all too easy to compare myself unfavourably with the great and the good, but one thing I did truly believe was that my brand of creativity was special to myself. I then thought of an evocative phrase that would encourage me and designed a poster featuring it. It contained the words: 'My creativity is uniquely my own'.

Next I used the power of imagery to see myself already owning the quality of connectedness through my creativity. I visualised people reading my next book (not yet written) and of being helped and inspired by it. I imagined them writing letters to me, and thought of my responses. The feelings associated with these reveries were warmly positive and would assist in preventing me from being daunted by such a huge task.

Finally, I asked a colleague to support me with my goal, which she readily agreed to do.

Have another look at Chapters 2 and 5 for a more detailed description of working with affirmative sentences and images. Select words and phrases that will encourage you and give you confidence, and visualise your goal as it will be when achieved. Use the Ideal Model technique, also described in Chapter 2, to inspire you.

5. Planning the programme

It is easy to become so carried away with the process of doing something, that the goal is never attained. How tempting it would be to spend all my spare time thinking up new ideas for books and elaborating on them, without involving myself in the hard grind of daily writing! One way of making sure that my next book would be finished was to find a publisher at the outset. The effort would then be collaborative in terms of synopsis and schedule and I would benefit from feedback from a good editor.

Having made this decision, the next task was to choose the theme that excited me most and which I genuinely wanted to share with others. How did I want to be connected with others through the medium of writing? Detailed planning of the book required much creativity and I used meditation to help me with this. Having completed some sample material, I sent it to my agent. At this stage I needed the humility to accept his criticisms and make recommended adjustments, but I trusted his judgement implicitly.

You will need pen and paper here to create your plan of action. How will you carry out the steps towards realising your aim, who with and in what situation? How long will it take? What resources are necessary? Is it realistic and practicable?

6. Carrying out the project

The attitude here is one of direction, of bringing all the elements together to achieve the desired goal. It is also concerned with having access to one's personal faculties, thoughts, feelings, sensations, intuition and imagination, and guiding them appropriately. As long as I tried to impose my will on the creative process, the book ground to a halt, either because of a block or because I became panic-stricken about falling behind the schedule. I needed to remind myself constantly that my intuition flourished best in a relaxed atmosphere, and that good ideas frequently came to me after pottering around the garden! Keeping the image of my readers in mind gave me the correct focus throughout and helped me to write in a personal and friendly way.

I also enlisted the aid of my subpersonalities. Mr Regulator was in his element as far as the schedule was concerned, while Ragamuffin had fun playing with words. Meanwhile, it was necessary to keep a watchful eye on Miss Whip in case she started to drive me too hard.

You are now the director of your production, which is the attainment of your goal. What personal qualities do you need to draw on? Which subpersonalities will assist you and which are likely to cause havoc? Use meditation and visualisation to support you. Have other people around you who are encouraging and helpful. Keep reminding yourself of the importance of this project and picture all those individuals who will ultimately benefit from it.

Chapter 8
Heaven in a Wild Flower

A spiritual treasure. Peak experiences.
Mysticism in everyday life. Inner peace.
Your unique beauty. The loving attitude.
The wisdom within.

'I am in search of a spiritual treasure, but I have no idea what it is or how I shall reach it.

'The sky is stormy, with heavy black clouds scudding along. I am huddled in a ditch by the bare roots of an old oak, my cloak drawn around me for protection. There are many big trees which bend and sway wildly in the wind. There is no one around and no sign of a path. There is little point in staying here, so the best option seems to be to scurry along the ditch. The sky darkens and after a while I begin to lose heart, especially as tiredness and hunger overtake me. It soon becomes a huge effort to put one foot in front of the other, but I know that I must go on.

'Eventually I see a light on the left flickering through the trees, and, with growing optimism, make my way towards it. There, in a clearing, is a tumbledown, stone-built cottage. By now I am desperate for warmth and shelter, so I knock on the door. An old man appears dressed in rags. He seems to recognise me and says, "Ah,

I've been expecting you", and waves me inside. He holds a lantern which he puts on the table, then offers me a slice of bread. A copper kettle gleams in the firelight, and when the water is boiled the man makes me a special brew which I drink gratefully.

'The black-and-white cat, which until now has been snoring gently by the hearth, stretches lazily and jumps nimbly on to my lap. At last I am beginning to feel warm and accepted, but I am curious to know why the old man has been expecting me. "You are a person in search of yourself", he says, "and this is part of your journey, but you can only rest here a little while. You can have the cat as your guide." "But which way do I go?" I enquire with some trepidation, and he replies, "Trust the animal to guide you."

'Reluctantly, I finish my warming brew. As he shakes my hand, I ask if I will see him again, but he simply looks into my eyes with kindness and understanding. The cat is waiting for me, so I thank the man and go.

'By now it is night time, but I feel exhilarated by the dark. The cat trots ahead of me, the white patches on its back and tail illuminating the way. The wind has dropped and everything is so quiet that I can hear the leaves crunch under my feet. I desperately want to know where I am going and what awaits me and attempt to ask the cat, but she is a mysterious animal, unable to speak. I just have to trust her.

'The moon comes up and visibility improves. There is a smell of salt in the air and I realise that we are approaching the sea. I feel expectant. We leave the forest behind us and the landscape opens out. Soon we find ourselves by the shore. The moonlight gleams on the water, illuminating the waves that lap gently over the sand. By now the cat has finished guiding me, so she turns away and I am on my own.

'The sea seems to invite me and I long to follow that silvery pathway. There is a piece of driftwood nearby, just large enough for myself, and I float away from the shore following the luminous way. There is a sense of peace as I use my hands to paddle along. The light is drawing me and I glide smoothly through the sea. After a while the raft moves more quickly until the front tilts and I find myself flying up into the air along a moonbeam. By now I am travelling very quickly and I can hear some glorious music.

'In a flash I realise that this is what I have been looking for – not an object, but the most beautiful sound in the world. I seem to be part of the sound, part of the vibration of the music, whether very high or very low. I am completely embraced by it.

'Now I have arrived at my destination and I experi-ence a wonderful sense of elation and oneness as my body dissolves into the eternal rhythms of the universe.'

As I came towards the end of this visualisation, it was almost impossible to put into words the profound sense of harmony and unity. I had read about such an experience in spiritual texts, but had never understood its meaning until then.

American psychologist Abraham Maslow set himself the task of examining healthy, fully functioning people who appeared to have lives that were totally satisfying. What were the ingredients that contributed to their sense of fulfilment? One very important component was their ability to allow themselves to have what he termed 'peak experiences', which were characterised by feelings of awe, wonder, elation, sudden illumination, seeing something afresh as if for the first time, a sense of the sacred within the worldly, a clear perception of timelessness, of universality. Such experiences provide a complete shift in perspective, are deeply meaningful to the person involved and are often described in spiritual terms.

Sadly, the prosaic, technological culture which predominates in the Western world offers little place for the mystical. Sublime experiences are generally considered to be of small worth and are therefore often suppressed. However, the fact remains that humans have a natural urge towards transcendence, a yearning to rise above and beyond the mundane. If you allow yourself to explore the transpersonal realm, your life will be greatly enriched. Here is your opportunity.

The treasure

First become deeply relaxed and acknowledge that this fantasy will lead you into a sublime domain.

You are in search of a spiritual treasure, something that will be profoundly significant to you. You find yourself in a particular landscape. Let your mind's eye fill in the details. Where are you? What is the atmosphere of this place? Do you have a sense of direction at this point? See what happens. Perhaps you need someone or something to guide you. If so, then notice who or what appears. Let a dialogue develop.

Continue on your route for as long as necessary and be aware of how the scenery changes. What are your feelings? Are there any obstacles? If so, what can help you overcome them?

Eventually you sense that you are coming towards your destination, the very spot where your treasure is hidden. What is its setting? How do you feel now? Perhaps a guardian watches over it. Are there any interactions? Be receptive to whatever occurs.

At last the moment arrives when you set eyes upon this most precious item. What is it? How do you respond? If you are in touch with the spiritual realm, allow yourself to savour the experience.

When you have opened your eyes, write a verse about your discovery.

My imaginary journey was symbolic of my early struggles through life and the depression I often suffered from. It also conveyed the sense of loss and alienation that sometimes affected me. The old man represented a mentor who was very helpful at a critical stage in my life and the cat was indicative of my intuition. The quality I most needed for myself on this spiritual quest was trust. I also needed to surrender myself to nature and to music, both of which put me in touch with the mystical sphere. How do you interpret your journey and what meanings do you find?

MYSTICISM IN EVERYDAY LIFE

You will need some space for movement in the following exercise.

Imagine that you are sitting at a table in a darkened room. You are about to meet a mystical being. A single candle burns and you are looking into the flame. You watch it flickering for a while. Many colours are visible in its halo of light: yellow, orange, blue, white . . . As you peer searchingly into the depths of the flame, an image begins to form of the mystical being. Gradually its features become clearer. You would like to get to know it better and take the opportunity to ask it about itself. How does it reply and what does it reveal about itself? What are your feelings towards it? Does it have a message for you? Let the dialogue continue.

You are now going to experience what it is like to be the Mystic. Step into its place and take on its form. What is that like? Begin to move around as the Mystic and make any appropriate sounds. Describe yourself. What special qualities do you have? How does the world appear to you? What are your feelings towards it and towards the people there? What gifts can you offer? What ideas and visions do you have?

When you have fully explored the Mystic, return to your place at the table and see the apparition fade into the candle flame.

Suddenly there is a knock on the door, someone enters and switches on the light. As you shield your eyes against the bright illumination, you are aware that a very down-to-earth practical character has entered. This is the Realist. What does this one look like? What is the body posture? The Realist wants to perform a task. What is that? How do you respond? Do you wish to open a conversation? Say whatever comes to you and listen to the replies.

Now switch into the role of the Realist. Is this easy? How do you now hold yourself and what is your expression? What feelings do you connect with? Is there anything that you need? Do you have any limitations? What are your attributes? What do you want to do? What would you most like to offer the world? Are any new qualities trying to come through?

Step out of the character and return to your place at the table. You watch the Realist exit through the door and you decide to follow. You find yourself in a meadow. To your surprise, both the Mystic and the Realist are here and they are talking earnestly together. How do they interact? Are there any ways in which the one can assist the other? Can the Mystic's dreams and visions be fulfilled with practical help from the Realist? Can you offer any suggestions?

Now explore these two subpersonalities through movement, identifying with first one and then the other, creating a dance. What is that like? How do the energies of each differ? What can each give the other?

Makes notes about what you have learnt.

As one sage said, 'Before enlightenment, chop wood, haul water. After enlightenment, chop wood, haul water.' While spiritual experiences can be of great value in themselves, it is always worth asking yourself how these can be manifest in the world. The mystical part may have great aspirations, but it will need the practical aspect to put these into action. Did you notice that the first was more about being and the second about doing?

The image I came up with for my Mystic was a large eagle which soared high in the sky far above the land. This gave me a different, broader perspective on life, providing the opportunity for deep insights. I was wild and free, in the sense of being closely in touch with nature; in fact I was part of it. I could trust the air to support me and allow myself to go with the flow. Here there were no struggles, and people's difficulties seemed distant. The drawback was that I lived in existential solitude.

The Realist appeared to me as an electric typewriter! This was an efficient, hard-working, responsible subpersonality who felt smug and clever, being able to keep to deadlines and make automatic corrections. Clickety clack, clack, clack: neat letters all in a row. I was very good at earning my living, but had a tendency to become stressed. There was also a tightness and rigidity there, although I was beginning to let go of some of the driven behaviour. The Realist needed to be more open to the insights of the Mystic and willing to offer suggestions for action.

INNER PEACE

Among my clients was a highly stressed sales executive called Jason. His job involved undertaking numerous long journeys on motorways, coping with fast, dense traffic. He was also responsible for a number of people working in his team, having to ensure that they were turning over business quickly enough, not to mention the constant worry of finding sufficient new outlets that would guarantee expansion. Jason craved for some kind of inner tranquillity, far away from the frantic rush and competition of business life. How could he find this? I guided him through the following fantasy.

The temple of peace

*Relax deeply and close your eyes. It is very early in the
morning, just as dawn is breaking and the birds are beginning to sing. You are walking down a street, which is
completely deserted. There is a crispness in the air. Soon
you come to a gateway which leads into a large park. As
you walk across the springy grass, worries and pressures
drift away from you. You pause for a while under a tall,
majestic tree, which is completely still. Calmness pervades
your whole being.*

*After a while a sweet perfume drifts towards you, and,
following the scent, you find yourself in a flower garden.
The early morning dew sparkles on the petals of roses and
lavender, the pastel colours blending softly together.*

*In the centre is a fishpond and you linger here to
watch the goldfish gracefully swimming among the reeds
and waterlilies.*

*A path leads you through some flowering shrubs. At
the end is a small gate which opens on to a Japanese garden
surrounded by slender bamboos. Some bellchimes tinkle
gently as you enter. The gravel is raked into a flowing
pattern, interrupted here and there by large flat stones and
boulders and an occasional earthenware pot containing the
diminutive figure of a bonsai tree. There is a sense of quiet
beauty and order and you rest here to contemplate the
varying textures and shapes. At the far end of the garden is
a small temple which seems to be surrounded by an aura of
light. You walk towards it and take off your shoes before
entering. You are aware that this is a sacred place. Inside,
it is cool and the light is low. As you sit here to meditate,
you are enveloped by a sense of eternal tranquillity and
peace. Stay here for as long as you wish.*

214

Before leaving, affirm to yourself that you will bring the quality of inner peace with you into the world.

After this meditation, Jason reported that he felt very much calmer. I encouraged him to stop for a few minutes each working day and take himself on an imaginative journey to the temple of peace, which he promised to do.

A wonderful aspect of visualisation is that you can do it absolutely anywhere and take a quick retreat from the hustle and bustle of everyday life. Just make sure that you are safe.

A thing of beauty

The visionary English poet William Blake (1757–1827) expressed both timelessness and beauty exquisitely in the following poem:

> To see the world in a grain of sand
> And heaven in a wild flower
> Hold infinity in the palm of your hand
> And Eternity in an hour.

Such experiences are available to everyone and are by no means exclusive to poets. However, poets are often more open to intensity of experience than the average person, either spontaneously or through the deliberate encouragement of a state of expanded consciousness. Dealing with everyday affairs normally demands the process of selective attention, which automatically causes our senses to exclude unnecessary input. This enables us to concentrate on the matter in hand and at the time is very useful. However, because we become so accustomed to this restricted field of awareness, we often forget to tune in to the miraculousness of the world around us. Opening one's eyes to beauty can provide incredible joy, as I discovered through a very simple exercise.

A group of us were asked to take a walk in the garden and return with an object of beauty, after which we were to place it on a cloth. We then spent some time studying our object, appreciating its special qualities and getting in touch with the very essence of its beauty. In doing this we connected imaginatively with those same faculties within ourselves.

I chose a white tulip. I was particularly struck by its fragility and grace. The fact that it was not quite perfect, because one leaf was bent, made it even more beautiful. The petals seemed to be almost luminous and delicately perfumed. Having overcome the embarrassment at acknowledging such features as part of me, I closed my eyes and tuned in to the qualities of the tulip within myself: my own grace, fragility and refinement. I also readily accepted my lack of perfection as a human being, but this meant that my best attributes shone all the more.

Find an object that represents beauty to you. It may be easier to choose a photograph or painting, and this is fine. Treat it with the reverence it deserves and place it on a cloth. Quietly contemplate the item and let yourself become fully receptive to its loveliness. Connect with the very essence of its beauty until it permeates your being.

Close your eyes and hold the image inside you. Does it have a message that tells you something about life? Very gently take on the spirit of the object. Stand up and move if this is helpful. Acknowledge that you, too, have such qualities. Connect with your own inner radiance. Promise yourself that you will let your unique beauty shine through in everyday life.

Write a poem about yourself and the object and the meaning it conveyed.

THE LOVING ATTITUDE

I have always been passionate about dancing. Moving with the flow of the music and forming myself into all kinds of shapes has always been hugely satisfying. Moreover, there is a wonderful sense of liberation about spinning and leaping across a large space.

I had just joined a new class and was immediately struck by the teacher, who, apart from her elegance and grace, seemed to emanate a natural warmth and radiance. Simply standing in her presence and conversing casually gave me a feeling of calm and reassurance. What was it about her that was so special? I noticed in particular her lack of anxiety and the openness of her expression. Everyone in the class seemed to grow and flourish spontaneously, not just from her excellent teaching, but because of who she was. Somehow, we knew intuitively that we could risk full exploration of ourselves through bodily movement, because whatever we did would be appreciated and accepted.

At the end of the class she gave each of us a flower, specially chosen from the vase she had brought with her. As she made this gesture, I realised that the quality this teacher had achieved was a loving attitude. Having put aside her own fears, she was able to give freely of her love, which was offered unconditionally. She seemed to perceive us as whole beings, for who we essentially were, and we in turn were able to blossom. What a priceless gift!

This sort of love is bountiful and self-generating. It is not limited by personal desires, nor is it dependent on the gratefulness of others. St Bernard expressed this succinctly: 'Love seeks no cause beyond itself and no limit; it is its own fruit, its own enjoyment. I love because I love; I love in order that I may love.' Not only are others blessed to receive this quality, but the giver also delights in it.

Bountiful love

This visualisation will help you to experience the love that seeks no reward. You may prefer to find a quiet place out of doors for this exercise.

You are walking up a hill in search of love, but your pace is slowed by the heavy bag you are carrying. You begin to realise that your quest is hopeless unless you can offload your burden. However, the bag is full of your worries, fears and anxieties, and you feel strangely attached to them. After all, you are well used to them by now, so who would you be without them? Yet you are becoming increasingly tired and yearn for lightness of being.

You sit down for a moment to reflect. You examine your bag carefully. What sort of bag is it? What is its size, its shape, its colour? What is it made of? Test its weight and consider how long you have had this burden. Open the bag and investigate its contents. What do you find?

You look around the landscape in search of a suitable

place to deposit your bag of worries, knowing that you can reclaim it later, after you have found the love that has no fear. What sort of place do you select? How do you feel when you say goodbye to your anxieties? How does the landscape now appear?

You continue on your journey with a light step and gladness in your heart. The sun shines warmly and a gentle breeze is blowing. You feel at peace with the world. By now you are approaching the brow of the hill, and on reaching the top, gasp with pleasure at the expansive view that is spread out before you. In the valley below, you can see scattered farms and houses, and the minute figures of people working in the fields. You sit down on the soft turf and open your heart to love. The sun is beginning to set and a pink glow radiates across the sky until you yourself are bathed in this warm light, the light of love. It permeates your innermost being. Stay with this experience for as long as you wish. As you look across the landscape you see that the whole valley is enveloped by the glowing light of love and you feel at one with everything.

Finally, it is time to make your return journey, but you take with you the gift of unconditional love. When you reclaim your bag, just notice whether it has changed at all.

INFINITE WISDOM

In my work with clients, I know that advice is generally not appropriate, nor can I provide the solutions to any of the problems. The best I can do is help people to find the answers themselves. In this process I trust absolutely that each individual has a source of inner wisdom that will point to the best way forward. All that is necessary is to have access to it. Indeed, it is perfectly possible to tap in to it at will, so whenever you feel stuck or confused, take yourself on an imaginative journey to meet your Sage and seek assistance.

The Sage

You are in a pretty meadow. It is early in the evening and the sun has just set. The air is warm and balmy and your mood is hopeful. You are looking forward to meeting this Sage or Wise Being because you have some pressing questions to ask. You consider what it is you need to know as the moon comes up. A track leading away from the meadow is now clearly illuminated and you decide to follow it.

The path takes you into a wood. Here the air is cooler and the pungent aroma of pine needles greets you. As you walk under the canopy of the trees, you feel tranquil and close to nature. You hear the sound of small creatures rustling in the undergrowth.

On the far side of the wood the path stops by a gate. You go through and find yourself at the foot of a mountain. You look around, unsure which direction to take, until your eye is drawn to a brilliant star low in the sky. Now you are clear that you must follow the star, so you begin to climb. The ascent becomes steeper and soon you are scrambling over boulders, yet you are intent on meeting the Sage and no obstacle deters you.

As you pause for breath you notice a flickering light and you decide to investigate. After pushing your way through some bushes you find yourself near a large cave. A fire illuminates the entrance with a warm glow. You sense that you have arrived at your destination and are filled with anticipation. This is where you will encounter your Sage. You thank your star for guiding you here.

A voice welcomes you and invites you into the cave. Here you meet a being of infinite wisdom, who cares deeply about you and knows what is best for you. You now have the opportunity to declare your troubles and ask whatever you wish. Let your conversation develop. How does the Sage reply? If there are no words, then maybe there is a sign or a gift.

You now feel wiser and some light has been thrown on your problem. The Sage assures you that you can come to the cave to ask for advice whenever you have the need. It is time to leave, so you say farewell and make your return journey down the mountain, locating the gate and the path through the wood, until you are once more in the meadow.

Make some notes about what you have discovered.

Afterword

If you have worked steadily through this book, you will by now understand yourself a great deal better and be more accepting of yourself. You will be well accustomed to using your imagination to help you overcome practical as well as emotional difficulties, and will realise that you have at your service a valuable tool that will assist with problems concerning relationships, poor health, work issues or just everyday worries. Moreover, you will have an appreciation of your potential, how you might bring that into being by using your will, and what life now holds in store for you. You may have been staggered by the vividness of your images and experienced liberating insights. Equally, part of this inner journey may have been confrontational or even a little frightening or confusing, presenting you with information that you find hard to deal with. If this is the case, then do seek help from a well-qualified therapist who is trained in the use of the imagination (*see* Useful Information).

Perhaps you have just dipped into the book here and there, as your fancy has taken you, and this is fine. However much or little you have used the visualisations, review what you have learnt and write a summary in your workbook. As a final exercise, make a drawing of a mandala.

AFTERWORD

The mandala

A mandala is an abstract circular drawing or painting that represents your innermost being, the whole of your psyche as you intuitively perceive it at present. It has about it a sense of unity and completeness.

Before picking up your pencil or brush, meditate on your essential nature, your self in its entirety, and allow the mandala to form in your mind's eye. Then let your hand represent it on paper.

You may decide to repeat this exercise on future occasions as a visual reminder of your personal transformation.

Remember: you have the resources inside yourself to guide you towards a fulfilling life. Trust in this and allow your intuition to speak to you.

Glossary

Affirmations Positive statements made about oneself to counteract negative beliefs and images, and to improve feelings of self-worth.

Anorexia nervosa A person suffering from anorexia has severe difficulty eating, to the point of starvation. This is a serious condition, which often affects adolescent girls and young women.

Bulimia In its literal sense, a state of morbid hunger. The sufferer may binge-eat, but then has a compulsion to empty the food out of the body, either by vomiting or laxatives.

Conscious Being in a state of awareness, in which one's mental faculties are awake.

Counsellor A person who is trained to offer guidance and support to people in need of help. Skills vary greatly according to qualifications, and can range from short-term befriending to in-depth, long-term work with people suffering from serious difficulties.

Gestalt An integrated whole. A form of psychology, mainly of perception, that originated in Germany in the 1930s and '40s. From this, Gestalt psychotherapy developed, which focuses on immediate experience and is characterised by particular techniques, such as the use of fantasy and metaphor, and imaginary dialogues.

Panic attack A state of extreme anxiety in which the person fears some impending disaster. This experience can be accompanied by symptoms such as nausea and dizziness.

Paranoia A mental disorder which features delusions of grandeur or persecution. The person generally has an abnormal tendency to suspect and mistrust others.

Phobia Extreme dread or uncontrollable fear of a particular object or situation.

Potential Lying dormant, but capable of coming into being.

Projection Attributing to other people characteristics which really belong to ourselves, but which we do not wish to acknowledge as ours. An unconscious defensive process.

Psyche From the Greek word meaning soul or spirit. Its meaning has broadened and now generally indicates the whole of one's essential nature.

Psychiatrist A doctor who specialises in treating mental illnesses. In the UK psychiatrists will focus on drug treatment, but in countries such as the USA they may also offer psychoanalysis or psychotherapeutic treatment.

Psychoanalysis A method of treatment of nervous and mental disorders, developed by Sigmund Freud, which particularly emphasises the influence of the unconscious. A patient may see their analyst several times a week for a number of years.

Psychologist A scientist who studies the nature of the mind. A clinical psychologist will generally work in a medical setting and assess and assist people with mental illnesses.

Psychosomatic An illness with physical symptoms but which is caused or aggravated by some kind of emotional or mental distress.

Psychosynthesis A method of psychotherapy founded by the Italian psychiatrist Roberto Assagioli, a student of both Freud and Jung. It is sometimes referred to as 'psychology with a soul', as it recognises the importance of spirit as well as mind and body. While examining past influences, it places particular emphasis on the realisation of potential.

Psychotherapy The treatment of emotional and mental disorders by psychological methods. In its traditional or 'psychodynamic' form, it accentuates developmental processes and past conditioning and considers how these influence current behaviour. It is generally a long-term form of therapy.

Subpersonality A part of the personality consisting of a cluster of thoughts and feelings which seems to have a life of its own. Discovery of one's subpersonalities is a useful technique for self-understanding.

Transpersonal Above or beyond the personal, often equated with the spiritual realm. A transpersonal psychology, such as psychosynthesis, incorporates the concept of Self or soul into its theory.

Unconscious Processes of which we are unaware. When used with the definite article, 'the unconscious', it usually indicates the structure underlying the personality, with which we are unacquainted but which influences behaviour in many ways.

References

1. This is a classic subpersonality exercise which I first experienced at the Psychosynthesis and Education Trust. A similar one can be found in *Psychosynthesis in Education* by Diana Whitmore (Turnstone Press, 1986), pp. 122–4.
2. My own version of an exercise learnt at the Trust and described in Diana Whitmore's book (as above), pp. 121–2.
3. Adapted from 'The Phobia Cure', described in *Introducing Neuro-Linguistic Programming* by Joseph O'Connor & John Seymour (Aquarian/HarperCollins, 1993), pp. 171–4.
4. Based on the paper 'Forgiveness – a teachable skill for creating and maintaining health' by G.A. Pettitt (available at the Psychosynthesis and Education Trust).
5. Another version of this exercise is printed in Diana Whitmore's book (as above), pp. 178–80.
6. Adapted from the exercise 'Purpose' by Piero Ferrucci, from his book *What We May Be* (Thorsons, 1995), pp. 72–4.

Answers to questions in Chapter 1:
b) One.
c) The three outer coins, forming the points of the triangle, are moved round to make up the outer corners of the inverted triangle.
d) A conundrum! Consider whether the downward pressure of the wings in flight counteracts the weight of the bird on the perch.

Bibliography

Assagioli, Roberto, *The Act of Will: A Guide to Self-Actualization and Self-Realization* (Turnstone Press, 1984).

Assagioli, Roberto, *Psychosynthesis* (Turnstone Press, 1965).

Charles, Rachel, *Mind, Body and Immunity: Enhancing Your Body's Natural Defences for Good Health and Long Life* (Cedar, 1990; 2nd edn 1996).

Ferrucci, Piero, *What We May Be: The Vision and Techniques of Psychosynthesis* (Thorsons, 1995).

Freud, Sigmund, *The Interpretation of Dreams,* trans. Strachey, James (George Allen & Unwin, 1954).

Gallwey, W.T., *The Inner Game of Tennis* (Pan, 1986)

Gawain, Shakti, *Creative Visualisation* (Bantam, 1982).

Glouberman, Dina, *Life Choices, Life Changes: The Art of Developing Personal Vision Through Imagework* (Thorsons, 1995).

Hadfield, J.A., *Dreams and Nightmares* (Penguin, 1954).

Hall, Eric and Carol, and Leech, Alison, *Scripted Fantasy in the Classroom* (Routledge, 1990).

Jeffers, Susan, *Feel the Fear and Do It Anyway* (Arrow, 1991)

Jung, Carl Gustav, Introd. Chodorow, Joan, *Jung on Active Imagination* (Routledge, 1997).

Jung, Carl Gustav, *Memories, Dreams, Reflections* (Fontana Press, 1995).

Koestler, Arthur, *The Act of Creation* (Arkana/Penguin, 1989).

Maslow, Abraham H., *Religions, Values and Peak-Experiences* (Penguin, 1976).

McClelland and Kirshnit, 'The effect of motivational arousal through film on saliva immunoglobulin-A', in *Psychology and Health*, 2 (1988), 31–52.

Satyananda, Swami, *Yoga Nidra* (Bihar School of Yoga, Munger Bihar, India, 1983).

Simonton, Carl O., Matthews-Simonton, Stephanie, and Creighton, James L., *Getting Well Again* (Bantam, 1986).

Whitmore, Diana, *Psychosynthesis Counselling in Action* (Sage, 1991).

Whitmore, Diana, *Psychosynthesis in Education, a Guide to the Joy of Learning* (Turnstone Press, 1986).

Whyte, Lancelot Law, *The Unconscious Before Freud* (Basic Books, Inc., 1960).

Useful information

A complete list of qualified counsellors can be obtained from the British Association for Counselling which covers all areas of the UK. It is best to select someone who is fully BAC accredited and UKRC registered. Fees are often on a sliding scale according to income and some counsellors offer an initial interview free or at a reduced rate. It is important to feel comfortable with the person and it is therefore customary to meet more than one counsellor in the first instance so that you can make a choice.

British Association for Counselling
1 Regent Place, Rugby, Warwickshire CV21 2PJ
Tel: 01788 578328

Psychosynthesis counsellors and therapists are trained at the following institutes in the UK, each of which has a referral service and provides low-cost counselling with supervised trainees. All graduates are able to work with guided visualisation.

The Psychosynthesis and Education Trust
92–94 Tooley Street, London Bridge, London SE1 2TH
Tel: 020 7403 7814 (referrals) or 020 7403 2100 (office)

The Institute of Psychosynthesis
65A Watford Way, Hendon, London NW4 3AQ
Tel: 020 8202 4525 (information)

USEFUL INFORMATION

The Association of Humanistic Psychology Practitioners can send you a list of qualified counsellors and psychotherapists who practise in a humanistic mode, including psychosynthesis and Gestalt.

The Association of Humanistic Psychology Practitioners
BCM AHPP, London WC1N 3XX
Tel: 0345 660326 (answerphone)

Mind is a national organisation in the UK offering help and guidance to people with mental and emotional problems. Your local centre will be listed in the telephone directory.

The Samaritans offers 24-hour telephone counselling to people in crisis and is listed in your local directory. This organisation will also put you in touch with agencies that give specialist support, for example with eating disorders or drug or alcohol problems.

Relate provides counselling for couples or individuals with relationship or marriage difficulties. The national headquarters will supply the address of your area referrals office.

Relate
Herbert Gray College, Little Church Street, Rugby
CV21 3AP
Tel: 01788 573241

The Society of Analytical Psychology will recommend a Jungian analyst in your area.

Society of Analytical Psychology
1 Daleham Gardens, London NW3 5BY
Tel: 020 7435 7696

The Women's Therapy Centre offers group and individual therapy for women suffering from eating disorders and other difficulties. This organisation can put you in touch with resources in your area, including individual counsellors and self-help groups.

Women's Therapy Centre
10 Manor Gardens, London N7 6JS
Tel: 020 7263 6200

AUSTRALIA

Institute of Applied Counselling
LVL 5/ 185 Elizabeth Street, Sydney 2000
Mobile service: 014 991 197. Tel: (02) 9261-8727

Institute of Counselling
190 High Street, Willoughby 2068, Sydney
Tel: (02) 9417-8352

Lifeline
24-hour crisis counselling, all areas: Tel: 13-1114.
Personal and couples counselling: Tel: (07) 3252 7086.
Office and counselling service: 310 Sydney Road, Sydney
Tel: (02) 9949 5522

Marriage Guidance Council
159 St Paul's Terrace, Queensland 4000
Tel: (07) 3831 2005
Help for families.

NEW ZEALAND

The Mental Health Foundation of New Zealand
62–64 Valley Road, Mt Eden, Auckland
Tel: 0–9–630 8573

Counselling and Psychotherapy Association
1 Thorndon Quay, Thorndon, Wellington
Tel: 0–4–499 1955

Lifeline
Crisis counselling, all areas. Call free on 0800 353 353.
PO Box 8045, Nelson
Tel: 0–3–546 8899

Institute of Psychosynthesis
7 Farnol Street, Hillsborough, Auckland 4
Tel: 0–9–625 9559
Psychosynthesis counselling and psychotherapy for all. Low-cost counselling by supervised trainees.

Marriage and Family Counselling Centre
34 Turongo Street, Otorohanga
Tel: 0–7–873 7535

CANADA

Counselling and Psychotherapy Services
2 Mount Royal, Hamilton, Ontario L8P 4H6
Tel: (905) 529–3480

EPRA – Ecole de Psychosynthèse et de Relation d'Aide
1338 Fleury E, Montrèal, Québec
Tel: 514 381–9681
Psychosynthesis counselling and training.

Marriage and Family Therapy Clinic
64 Queen, St Catharines, Ontario L2R 5G7
Tel: (905) 687–6866

**Ontario Association for Marriage
and Family Therapy**
Tel: 1–800–267–2638 (toll-free)

Psychotherapy Institute and Counselling Clinic
120 Carlton, Toronto, Ontario
Tel: (416) 968–0640 (toll-free)

UNITED STATES OF AMERICA

Psychosynthesis Palo Alto
461 Hawthorne Avenue, Palo Alto, California, CA 94301
Tel: (415) 321 6562

New York Center for Psychotherapy
1155 Park Avenue, New York, NY 10128–1209

Index

*Figures in **bold** type denote visualisation exercises.*

symbolism 6, 9, 15, 21
  of dreams 182
  of food 97, 98
  of illness **93**
  meaning of 17
  supportive 152

thoughts 20, 25, 35, 38
  awareness of 113
  clusters of 28, 33
  conflicting 19
  difficult 109, 112, 126
  disclosure of 114
  expression of 117, 123
  guiding 204
  honesty with 113
  intrusive 14
  positive **106**
time 146, 167, 168
  machine **162–4**
  quality 105, 125
  relationship to 109–10, **146–8**
tranquillity 43, **62**, **65**, **75**
  inner 213, 214
transformation 48, 102, 223
  of subpersonalities 38, **40–1**
transpersonal 209, 226
  and the will 191
trauma 11, 130

unconscious 3, 4, 8, 9, 10, 12, 15, 16, 28, 31, 169, 172, 226
  apprehension about 7
  collective 9
  and dreams 181, 183
  force 190
  images from 5, 21–2, 153, **159**
  messages from 16
  wealth in 6

what it is 8
understanding:
  need for 39, 107
  of others **106**, **110**, 111, 117, 131, 135
  reflecting back **107**
  of self 9, 28, 38
  of subpersonality 40
unhappiness **46**, 50, 68, 172

vision 27, **211**
  of future 167, **168–9**, **171**
  of potential 173
  realisation of 172, 212
  of self 48, **98**, **169**
visualisation 5, 9, 14, 15, 19
  difficulties with 10–11
  interpreting 15
  learnings from 222
  practice of 7, **11–12**, 12–17
  tape-recording of 13, 14
vulnerability **93**, 126, 127, 142

wholeness 27, 28, 38
will 51, 184, 185, **186–7**, 194, 195, 198
  act of 199–205
  engagement of the 17
  good **125**, **126**, 190, **191**
  imposing 204
  skilful 188–9, **189–90**
  strong **187–8**
  transpersonal 191–3, **193–4**
willingness **198–9**
wisdom 6, 40, **219–21**
wise being 9, **128**, **220–1**
work 82, 83, 107, 137–41, **138–9**, 150, 152, 154, 168
worry 213, **218–19**
  see also anxiety
writing 10, 15, 27, 33, 35, 51
  to express feelings 118

If you would like to contact the author for further information please write to:

Rachel Charles

c/o Piatkus Books
5 Windmill Street
London
W1P 1HF